O Love That
Not Let Me G

Ian Campbell Bradley was born in 1950 and educated at New College, Oxford, where he took a first-class degree in modern history and completed a doctorate on nineteenth-century religion and politics. After a career as a journalist with the BBC and *The Times* and a period as a schoolmaster, he studied at St Andrews University where he obtained a first-class degree in divinity. He served as Assistant Minister of St Leonard's Parish Church, St Andrews, and is now Head of Religious Programmes for BBC Scotland. An experienced writer and broadcaster, his previous books include *The Strange Rebirth of Liberal Britain, Enlightened Entrepreneurs* and *God is Green*, a study of Christianity and the environment. He is also the editor of the *Penguin Book of Hymns*.

O Love That Wilt Not Let Me Go

Meditations, prayers
and poems

by George Matheson

Selected and introduced

by Ian Campbell Bradley

Collins
FOUNT PAPERBACKS

First published in Great Britain by
Fount Paperbacks, London in 1990

Copyright © Ian Campbell Bradley

Typeset by Avocet Robinson, Buckingham
Printed and bound in Great Britain by
William Collins Sons & Co. Ltd, Glasgow

For Andrew David Bradley, at whose
baptism we sang
"O Love that wilt not let me go"

Contents

Preface

I know that I am not the only person to find George Matheson's "O Love that wilt not let me go" one of the most profound and moving hymns in the English language. It is frequently requested on BBC television's *Songs of Praise* and often heard on the radio programme *Sunday Half Hour*. Whenever I have used the hymn in a church service, several people have always come up at the end and told me how much it means to them. For at least one person I know the hymn has been instrumental in bringing about an awakening of interest in the Christian faith.

It was a desire to know more about the author of the words which have stirred so many that started me on a quest to find out something of George Matheson's life and his other writings. It has been a moving and enriching experience. I have found my own faith both deepened and challenged by reflecting on the life of this Victorian Scottish minister and reading his poems, meditations and prayers. They have a remarkable freshness and directness, and often too a striking note of modernity, even though they were written as much as a century ago. In October 1988 I included some of them in a radio programme in the BBC's *Seeds of Faith* series. A number of listeners wrote to me asking where they could find Matheson's devotional writings in print. The answer, until the publication of this book, was that they couldn't. The many volumes of his meditations which were published and republished around the turn of the century have long since been out of print. The selection from them that appears in the second half of this book will, I hope, help to re-establish the reputation of a man who has been unjustly neglected since his death more than eighty years ago.

Altogether George Matheson wrote over 800 devotional meditations and 100 poems. The small selection included here can hardly hope to be comprehensive, or even representative of this vast output, but I hope that it gives at least some indication of the breadth of themes that he covered and the catholicity of his thought. I have grouped the individual meditations and poems into ten sections each based around a single theme. They seem to me to reflect the dominant motifs in Matheson's theology and spirituality.

In keeping with his aim of resting feelings on thoughts (see pages 29–30), Matheson cast all his meditations in two-part form. The first part always aimed at suggesting or provoking a thought or reflection and the second part consisted of a short prayer. I have included several of the meditations in their original form but I have sometimes taken either just the initial piece of reflection or the prayer on its own. In every case I have appended Matheson's original title for each piece and the Biblical verse which inspired it. I have occasionally shortened meditations where they became slightly repetitive.

Most of what you will read in the pages that follow was originally intended to be read in church in place of the more conventional readings from the Scriptures. I have found that George Matheson's meditations work equally well as personal devotions but it would also be good to hear them used in church services.

IAN CAMPBELL BRADLEY

George Matheson: The Eyes of Faith and Imagination

George Matheson should surely stand alongside Thomas Chalmers and Lord George Macleod as one of the intellectual and spiritual giants in the post-Reformation Scottish Church. The breadth and volume of his published work is considerable, encompassing academic theology, popular poetry, devotional meditations on Biblical texts and prayers. As well as being a formidable scholar and brilliant writer, he was also an outstanding preacher and exemplary pastor. He spent his entire working life in the parish ministry of the Church of Scotland, unstintingly caring for the spiritual needs of his congregation and painstakingly preparing public worship Sunday after Sunday. All this despite the fact that he was blind throughout his adult life.

Matheson's blindness was almost certainly the single most powerful influence on his personality and his writings. It determined his choice of career and powerfully stimulated his powers of imagination. Blindness was a particularly cruel handicap for one who had a passionate love of books and reading, a great desire for human company and a deep attachment to the beauties of nature. Although he uncomplainingly accepted his disability, it caused him much private anguish and brought him periods of intense loneliness. It also led him to ask questions about the suffering of the innocent and at times severely tried his faith in a loving God. Yet that faith was never destroyed and ultimately perhaps it was even deepened. Matheson's blindness strengthened the power of his imagination and highlighted the element of sacrifice which he saw as standing at the heart of the Christian mystery.

George Matheson was born in Glasgow on 27 March 1842, just five years after the accession of Queen Victoria. His father, also called George, hailed from Dornoch in Sutherland and was proud of his Highland blood. He had originally intended to become a minister and went to Glasgow University where he was a proficient classical scholar but on the advice of friends he took up a career in business and became a leading merchant and wholesale warehouseman in Glasgow. He married a second cousin and they had eight children of whom George junior was the second.

Young George was only eighteen months old when his mother realized that there was something wrong with his eyesight. The cause was found to be inflammation at the back of the eyes, a condition which at that time was incurable. Throughout his childhood he suffered from gradually fading vision. For most of his schooldays, which were spent in a succession of small private schools and then at Glasgow Academy, he could see well enough to read and write provided he wore powerful spectacles and sat by a window to get full advantage of the sunlight. But by the time he went up to Glasgow University in 1857 he was dependent on others reading to him and by the age of eighteen he was effectively blind. Just occasionally in later life he would have periods of partial vision: sometimes when he was in his manse at Innellan if the light was particularly good he could dimly make out the shapes of the steamers plying up and down the Clyde. But apart from these few brief moments, he spent his entire adult life in a world of darkness and isolation.

Despite this terrible handicap, Matheson had a brilliant academic career. He was a lively and perhaps even a slightly precocious child. At the age of seven he was preaching a sermon to the rest of the family, standing on a chair with a couple of strips of paper pinned to his chest in imitation of the Geneva bands worn by Church of Scotland ministers. In fact, his original desire was to become a lawyer but his fading sight ruled out that career and he decided instead to opt for the ministry. He entered Glasgow University at the early age of 15 and spent a total of nine years there, studying first Arts and then Divinity.

As a student, despite his rapidly fading sight, he was neither introverted nor shy. A contemporary recalled that "his laughter was the biggest and heartiest in the College quadrangle, being equalled, however, by his tenderness and sensibility". He had a particular fondness for singing, with "D'ye ken John Peel", "The harp that once through Tara's halls" and "Believe me if all those endearing young charms" being favourites in his repertoire. He also showed his budding talents as a poet, completing two long epic poems in his early student days, one on the Flood and the other about a blind girl in classical Greece.

In 1866 he was licensed by the Glasgow Presbytery and he served his assistantship in Trinity Parish Church in the Sandyford district of the city. The minister there, John Ross MacDuff, was also to achieve some fame as a hymn writer – his "Christ is coming! Let creation from her groans and travails cease" is still to be found in several hymnbooks. But it is unlikely that the young assistant learned much from his senior about the art of hymn writing as MacDuff was away in the Holy Land for a good deal of the time that Matheson was attached to his church.

In 1868 George Matheson was ordained into the charge of Innellan in Argyllshire. This small coastal town which stands further down the Cowal Peninsula from Dunoon and across the Firth of Clyde from Wemyss Bay was a popular Victorian tourist resort and the Matheson family had long taken their summer holidays there. His ministry there, which lasted for eighteen years, centred on preaching and he devoted a good deal of time to preparing his Sunday morning sermons. He began on the previous Sunday afternoon when he selected his text which he then pondered over during the early part of the week. On Wednesday he would begin dictating his sermon, usually to his sister who lived with him, and by Saturday morning he would have it finished. The sermons generally ran to about twenty minutes. Until 1878 he committed them entirely to memory but thereafter he simply prepared an outline sketch from which he preached.

By all accounts Matheson's performance in the pulpit was masterly. His use of language was strikingly fresh and original and he had that sense of timing and of the dramatic gesture and pause which is so essential to the preacher as well as the actor. He memorized not just his sermons but also his prayers and the Bible readings for the day. These last he appeared to read out of the pulpit Bible which was always left open in front of him. When preaching, he gave the impression of looking the congregation full in the face and many visitors to his church came away from the service with no idea of his blindness. In an age when preachers were viewed rather as pop stars and footballers are in our own time, Matheson drew visitors from far and wide to Innellan and was regarded as one of the town's main tourist attractions. Several people took their holidays there largely to hear him preach and stopped coming when he left.

Matheson gripped his congregation through his prayers as well as in his sermons. One of those who regularly worshipped at his church and who himself went on to become a minister has left this vivid account of the start of his services:

Dr Matheson's first prayer was often the finest part of the service. And what a prayer it was! A lifting up of the heart and upraising of the spirit, a reaching out after God, an outpouring of the soul, like the rapturous song of the lark, mounting higher and higher into the blue, to

17

find in the limitless skies the satisfaction of its whole nature. I confess that it was this first prayer that often lifted us up into the Mystic Presence more than any other part of the service. How difficult it was to keep the eyes closed! There, upon the high pulpit, was the blind poet, with uplifted hand, always reaching out and up into his own illumined darkness, as if trying to catch something of the mystery of God and draw it down to man. He carried us all up into the heights along with him; and he drew down, for the most commonplace of us, something of the transfiguring blessing; so that, often before the rapture of aspiration was over, the eyes that watched the blind, praying man in the pulpit had to view him through a mist of unconscious tears.

Although the ministry of the word was at the heart of his work in Innellan, George Matheson did not neglect the pastoral side of his calling. He was a tireless visitor of the sick and housebound. A local doctor wrote after he left "seldom have I seen a clergyman so near the heart of his parishioners, not merely in prosperity and success – that is easy and hardly wanted – but in sorrow and distress, in health and disease, in work and worship".

In 1885 Mattheson was summoned to preach before Queen Victoria at Crathie Church next to Balmoral Castle. He took as his theme the prophet Job's endurance of repeated and overwhelming calamities. His portrayal of Job as standing before the mysteries of life in a spirit of patient trust and hope deeply affected the queen and she requested that the sermon be printed for distribution around the Royal Household. Perhaps because of his own sufferings, he often found inspiration from the Book of Job for his prayers and meditations, as in the opening prayer in this collection (I. 1).

The year after his visit to Balmoral, the congregation of St Bernard's Church in the fashionable New Town area of Edinburgh called Matheson to be their next minister. Although he was sad to leave Innellan, he could not resist this invitation from one of the largest and most prestigious churches in the capital. For the next thirteen years he preached to packed congregations which included university professors and students, eminent lawyers, fellow clergymen and other notables of the city. As at Innellan, he was not just content with being a preacher and devoted much effort to pastoral matters. In the first six months of his ministry he personally visited the home of every member of the church – a total of over 1500 people. Throughout his time at St Bernard's he ran Bible classes and took an active interest in the numerous organizations attached to the church. In accordance with the general practice of the time, he generally carried out baptisms and marriages at his own house in the New Town at eight o'clock in the evening.

During his Edinburgh ministry and for several years after he had retired Matheson was in constant demand to preach all over Britain. He made a habit of visiting another church one Sunday each month and often his travels took him south of the border or into Wales. He was always careful to have several practices at climbing up into the pulpit of a strange church and making sure that there were no protruding gas lamps or other objects which he might hit with one of the hand gestures which invariably accompanied his sermons.

Four years after becoming minister at St Bernard's Matheson finally got round to learning Braille, or at least devising his own version of it. He also learned how to use a typewriter. This meant that he could write out his sermons, articles and books himself and did not have to dictate them to others. However, he was still dependent on his long-suffering sisters for reading books and papers. He also employed a series of secretaries to help in this task. William Smith, who took on this job for the last ten years of Matheson's life, when he had retired from the parish ministry, has left a record of a typical day. He would rise shortly before nine and take his breakfast while his letters and extracts from the morning papers were read out to him. He was particularly interested in book reviews, political stories and reports of criminal trials and also liked to be kept informed of new scientific and mechanical inventions. The rest of the morning was taken up by studying French and German, reading works of theology, philosophy, science, history and literature and then an hour or so of writing before lunch. There was more reading in the afternoon and a lighter diet of fiction in the evening. Often it was not until nearly midnight that the weary reader was allowed to put the last book down.

The demands that George Matheson made on

his secretaries and on his sisters were considerable. He came to depend on the latter particularly for companionship. He never married and as far as I can establish never came near to doing so. Certain old hymnal companions suggest that he wrote "O love that wilt not let me go" in a mood of acute depression after the girl that he loved had declined his proposal of marriage because of his blindness. This seems to be an entirely apocryphal story. The event that triggered the hymn seems to have been the marriage in the summer of 1881 of one of his sisters who had come with him to Innellan to be his housekeeper, reader, amanuensis and companion. The rest of the family were in Glasgow following the wedding and he found himself alone in the large manse, with just the sound of the sea outside for company. He later wrote of the verses that he penned at that time:

It is the quickest composition I ever achieved. It was done in three minutes. It seemed to me at the time as if someone was dictating the thought to me, and also giving the expression. There was so little sense of effort that I had a sensation of passiveness. I was sitting alone in my study in a state of great depression, caused by a real calamity. My hymn was the voice of my depression. It was not made for utilitarian purposes; it was wrung out spontaneously from the heart.

In fact, Matheson was not to be without a companion for long. Two other unmarried sisters took turns to look after him and both lived with

21

him in Edinburgh. Indeed, there does not seem to have been any substantial period of his life when he lived on his own. Nonetheless his blindness often gave him a feeling of solitude and his meditations on this subject, like those on the theme of getting old, are amongst the most sensitive and moving of all his writings (sections VII & VIII in the selection that follows).

Matheson retired as full-time minister at St Benard's in 1897 but remained for another two years as the regular preacher there. In retirement he continued to tour the country preaching and also to pour out a steady stream of books, articles and poems. Right up to the end his energy was prodigious. He spent the last days of his life in North Berwick, the East coast resort near Edinburgh where he had taken his summer holidays for many years. On the afternoon of 27 August 1906 he had a two and a half hour carriage drive and then settled down to an evening's reading which included a volume of the *Cambridge Modern History* and a novel. At 11.15 pm he was about to start working on his current project, a book about women in the Bible, but William Smith managed to persuade him to go to bed. At 1.30 in the morning of 28 August his sisters heard a slight moan. Shortly afterwards he died peacefully. He was buried in the family vault in the Glasgow Necropolis after a service that was attended by many of the city's leading civic and religious dignitaries.

The above brief account of Matheson's career as a minister may have suggested a man who went through life unassailed by doubts or uncertainties. In fact, he experienced a profound crisis of faith when he came very near to abandoning his ministry. Shortly after his ordination, he found that he had become, in his own words, "an absolute atheist. I believed in nothing, neither God nor immortality." The experience of having weekly to present the faith in which he had been brought up had suddenly made him feel that there was nothing there. He tendered his resignation to the Presbytery but it was wisely rejected on the grounds that he was a young man and would change his views.

He did change and in so doing broadened his faith in a way that helped him to relate in a very direct way to those who were not Christians. During his time at St Bernard's Matheson's sermons had a particular appeal to agnostics and to those who were themselves wrestling with doubts and uncertainties. There was nothing in him of the dogmatist or the narrow take-it-or-leave it Christian. Rather he was ever-open to those of other religions and of none and constantly striving to present his own faith in a way that was compatible with the principles of reason and the discoveries of science.

Matheson was helped out of his own crisis of faith by reading the works of the great German liberal theologians of the nineteenth century who had themselves been assailed with grave doubts about Christianity and had sought to reinterpret it in the light of post-Enlightenment philosophy. He was, in particular, deeply influenced by the writings of G. W. F. Hegel, who saw a deep and mysterious Spirit underlying all history and reconciling the self-contradictions that permeate every aspect of human experience. For Matheson that Spirit was Christianity, something that was built into the heart of man and that had existed from all time, long before the historic Christ came on the earth. Only in the light of its path of sacrifice and its message of love could the world and human life with all its vicissitudes and uncertainties be understood.

Matheson's interest in German philosophy and theology provided the subject of his first book, *Aids to the Study of German Theology*, which appeared in 1874 and in which he presented the ideas of such figures as Immanuel Kant, Friedrich Schleiermacher and David Friedrich Strauss not, as they had so often been presented to British readers, as negative and destructive of Christianity, but rather as rescuing and restating it in a way acceptable to modern scientific and rational minds. The thought of Hegel was an even more direct inspiration for his second work, *The Growth of the Spirit of Christianity* (1877) which explored two themes to which he was to return again and again in his writings, the doctrine of evolution and the integration of all religious faiths. Christianity, he argued, was the driving spiritual force throughout the history of the world, subject to the law of evolution and gradually unfolding more and more of its inner purpose. The pagan religions and Judaism he saw as its precursors, stages in the progressive revelation of God's great and mysterious being.

Matheson's third book, *Natural Elements of Revealed Theology*, was published in 1881. A strong believer in the idea of natural theology, he argued that there was something innately religious about human beings and that Christianity in many ways squared with their rational capacities. He believed that the German theologians and philosophers had successfully synthesized reason and revelation. "God's revelation", he wrote, "is the poetic form of natural reason." It was only possible because there was something in common between the Divine and the human – the fact of the Incarnation that enables communion between God and his creatures.

In 1885 Matheson published another book attempting to synthesize the worlds of religion and science, *Can the Old Faith Live with the New?* The new faith in question was the doctrine of evolution, with which like so many of his mid-Victorian contemporaries he was fascinated. For him it posed no challenge to the Christian faith, but rather deepened it. He was almost certainly influenced by the ideas of Henry Drummond, professor of Natural Science at the Free Church College in Glasgow, who had in 1883 published an influential book entitled *Natural Law in the Spiritual World*, which used the language of biology to illuminate the Christian message. In similar vein, Matheson cast Christ in evolutionary terms, drawing on the Biblical image of the second Adam to portray him as the summation and completion of humanity – the point to which we are all striving. It is an argument which in a remarkable way anticipates the evolutionary theology of Pierre Teilhard de Chardin in the middle of the twentieth century.

The same desire to reconcile the spirit of

Christian faith and the outlook of modern science underlay his next book, *The Psalmist and the Scientist* (1887). His essential instincts as a synthesizer and reconciler of apparently conflicting positions are also very evident in his important work on *The Distinctive Messages of the Old Religions*, which came out in 1892. I have included a brief extract from it in the selection that follows (IX, 2). Here he argues forcefully the point that is brought out so well in his great poem, "Gather us in, Thou Love that fillest all" (IX, 3), that the mission of Christianity is not to destroy or even replace the other great religions of the world, but rather to embrace and gather them in so that, as St Paul puts it in his first Epistle to the Ephesians, 1:10, all things shall be one in Christ.

George Matheson's strong sense that Christianity summed up the spirit of all religions is very much in the tradition of nineteenth-century German liberal Protestant theology as exemplified by such figures as Ernst Troeltsch and Adolf von Harnack. It also reflects the considerable interest in comparative religion in late Victorian Britain that followed the pioneering work of Max Muller, Professor of Sanskrit at Oxford, who edited fifty volumes of sacred texts from the East and believed that all the great religions of the world manifested a single principle. But by the standards of his contemporaries, Matheson was strikingly open and inclusive in his approach to other faiths and his assertion that "Thy presence is wider than our creed" (III, 6). In many ways, it is reminiscent of the doctrine of anonymous Christianity developed in our own age by the Roman Catholic theologian, Karl Rahner. It is not surprising that he was criticized for his extreme catholicity of belief and readiness to leap over not just denominational differences but the barriers between rival faiths. His writings show a tendency not just towards syncretism but also towards a doctrine of universal salvation. There is certainly not a hint in them of the Calvinist doctrines of election and predestination which figure prominently in the Westminister Confession of Faith to which as a Church of Scotland minister he had to subscribe at his ordiantion. It would be interesting to know what he thought of the fate of his near-contemporary, John McLeod Campbell, who was thrown out of the Church of Scotland in 1831 for his heretical stance in preaching a doctrine of universal atonement.

Matheson's other books were more Biblical and biographical in their themes. In 1888 he produced *Landmarks of New Testament Morality*, a treatise on Christian ethics, and in 1890 a study of *The Spiritual Development of St Paul*. There are interesting elements of his own personality and experiences in this latter work. Significantly he identified the thorn in the flesh which St Paul mentions in 2 Corinthians 12:7 as defective eyesight and portrayed the apostle as finding Jesus not through seeing him, as his disciples had, but through faith. The whole book is permeated with a sense of perfection achieved through suffering and with the idea of affliction as a means of spiritual growth – a theme which he took to be the central message of the Cross.

In 1896 Matheson published what is in many ways his most powerful and original book, *The Lady Ecclesia*, which he described as a spiritual biography. It is entirely allegorical in character and portrays the development of the Spirit of Christ in both the Church and the individual. In a vivid piece of imagery that he also used in several of his devotional meditations (for example IV, 2) he describes the kingdom which the Lady Ecclesia has inherited as an island, surrounded by the ocean and cut off from other communities and institutions.

Matheson's last years were particularly fruitful for his writing. In 1899 and 1900 he brought out two volumes of *Studies of the Portrait of Christ* and in 1902 four volumes on *The Representative Men of the Bible*, in which he produced pen portraits of figures who pointed up particular themes and phases in the Scriptures. At the time of his death he was working on a companion volume about women in the Bible.

Apart from these theological and biographical works, Matheson published eight volumes of devotional meditations and a book of poems. It is from them that the selection of his work that appears later in this book has largely been chosen. They are for me the finest products of a mind that displayed not just intellectual acuteness but also immense spiritual sensitivity and quite remarkable powers of imagination.

At a comparatively early stage of his ministry in Innellan Matheson had abandoned the traditional practice of reading two lessons from the Bible in the morning service. Instead he gave his congregation a meditation on a verse from the Scriptures. This practice was very popular and many of his congregation urged him to publish the meditations. It was not until 1882 that the first collection appeared under the title *My Aspirations*. The book was an instant success, going into numerous editions and finding its way into many homes not just in Scotland, but throughout Britain and on the Continent. A second volume of devotions, *Moments on the Mount*, was published in 1884. A third, *Voices of the Spirit*, appeared in 1888, followed by *Searchings in the Silence* (1895), *Words by the Wayside* (1896), *Times of Retirement* (1901), *Leaves for Quiet Hours* (1904) and *Rests by the River* which was published shortly before Matheson's death in 1906. All went into several editions and several were translated into German and achieved significant sales on the Continent as well as throughout Britain.

Matheson believed very strongly that devotional writing should have intellectual weight as well as spiritual depth. He had no time for the shallow emotionalism of much popular piety. "By devotional moments", he wrote in the preface to *Rests by the River*, "I do not mean moments of vacuity." Earlier, in the preface to *Times of Retirement* he had challenged the common view that devotion is a thing of the heart.

I do not think it is either merely or mainly so. I hold that all devotion is based upon intellectual conviction . . . The devotional writer must have a message as much as the

29

expositor. Devotion must be the child of reflection; it may rise on wings, but they must be the wings of thought. The meditations of this little book will appeal to the instinct of prayer just in proportion as they appeal to the teaching of experience; therefore before all things I have endeavoured to base the feeling of the heart on the conclusions of the mind.

Matheson's poems were gathered together into a volume of Sacred Songs in 1889. The two hymns for which he is known today, "O love that wilt not let me go" (X, 7) and "Make me a captive, Lord, and then I shall be free" (VI, 3), come from this collection. Like another great Victorian Christian and poet whose work he much admired, John Henry Newman, Matheson did not intend his verses to be sung as hymns. Indeed, they do not fulfil the criterion which he himself set for good hymns which is that they should abandon doctrine and concentrate on sounding a humanitarian note.

I don't think our hymns will ever be what they ought to be until we get them inspired by a sense of the enthusiasm of and for humanity. The hymnists speak of the surrender to Christ. They forget that Christ is not simply an individual. He is Head of a body, the body of humanity; and it no longer expresses the idea correctly to join yourself to Christ only, you must give yourself to the whole brotherhood of man to fulfil the idea. Hymnology is feeble and ineffective when it ignores the humanitarian side of religion.

In stressing the importance of humanitarianism in the Christian religion. Matheson was once again following the lead of German theologians like von Harnack and was very much in the mainstream of nineteenth-century Liberal protestantism. He often referred to Jesus Christ as being at the head of a "League of Pity" and made frequent references to practical charity in his devotional meditations, as in his remark about the Celestial City being a home for hospital training (II, 2). For all his superb intellectual powers and almost mystical imagination, he had a great sense of the practical side of the Christian Gospel and of the need for followers of Jesus to "quit the glorious mountain for the common plain" (V, 1) and "leave the green fields of speculation for the thorny paths of practice" (V, 4). I have included some of his meditations on this theme in the section entitled "The Christian Life".

The most striking characteristic of Matheson's meditations and poems is not their humanitarianism, however, but rather their originality. Again and again he takes a familiar passage from the Bible and gives it a wholly new interpretation, as in his use of the story of the shepherds and the wise men at the Nativity to distinguish two different kinds of Christian (V, 5). The key to the effectiveness of his devotional writings lies in his quite extraordinary powers of imagination. He had the ability to paint vivid impressionistic thought pictures to bring out the meaning of a Scriptural passage or a theological doctrine. In the words of a friend and fellow-minister:

All his work, written or spoken, was a transcription of what he mentally saw. Truth came to him in a vision; he did not reason it out . . . . His power lay in holding up to others the same living impression of a subject which he himself had experienced. His preaching was not so much the elucidation of a text or of a theme as the re-telling of a series of graphic impressions which the subject had already made on him. Hence also his writings assumed a descriptive rather than an argumentative form, and became by preference a series of protraits or picture studies.

At first sight, it might seem a strange paradox that this highly pictorial and impressionistic style of writing should be found in a man who was blind. Yet it was surely the fact of Matheson's blindness that greatly increased his power to make images in his mind which he then transferred to paper. If he was to see things he had to conjure them up in his mind's eye.

Like many blind people, he developed his other senses to compensate in part for his loss of visual perception. His sense of hearing was particularly acute. A close friend commented that it was "observing, discerning and thinking, the one perfect avenue in which things external poured into his thoughtful mind. In conversation the minutest difference of tone he at once detected. Many unknown people's peculiarities he diagnosed from their cough, their walk, their mode of blowing their noses". There is a particularly vivid illustration of how he used his hearing to stimulate his imagination in the story that a local doctor recounted of an evening spent with him in the manse at Innellan. A strong breeze was blowing over the Clyde outside throwing up white horses that broke on the shore with a muffled roar and a steamer was sounding its horn as it passed down the water. Standing by the window, the blind minister commented to his companion:

That weird music comes up here from the ocean like the far-off music of another world, a symphony of great Nature. How varied and multiform it is! I often listen to it, when sitting here alone, or perhaps sometimes in the depth of night; it puts one in reverie. And that? Listen! The monotone of that passing steamer, decisive and clear, how finely it blends with Nature's majestic music . . . . It reminds me of the story of Goethe when he was on the Alps. On the whole, it seemed he liked best not the mountains with their snowy peaks in the sky, but a manufactory in one of the valleys. The unceasing humming of the spinning-wheel sounded in his ears in such a place, as never before, as the Music of the Spheres. So is that symphony of Nature we are listening to, with the occasional syren-note.

Matheson's own thoughts on the need for blind people to cultivate and stimulate their powers of imagination are revealed in some remarks that he once made about deficiencies in their training: "They have been taught any amount of cyphering and manual work, but it seems to me they have not been taught what they most need, namely, how to conceive the thing that has been denied to them. The blind cannot conceive sight as sight but I hold that they may be able to conceive it by analogy''. He went on to suggest that by using sound and touch to convey the ideas of space, distance and even colour, it was possible to describe meaningfully to blind people even a process as apparently visual as the rising or setting of the sun.

In her book on the subject (*Imagination*, published in 1976), the philosopher Mary Warnock defines imagination as the power to produce images in the absence of the objects themselves imagined. If this is the case, then perhaps the blind are in a better position than the rest of us to develop this particular human faculty to the full. As she points out, seeing in the mind's eye may be more powerful than seeing in reality because we can concentrate on those images which are meaningful. ''The feeling engendered by the image may be more powerful in the absence than in the presence of the object.'' For a blind person this absence from objects is, of course, a permanent condition which must surely make the task of imaging, or imagining, more important than for a sighted person. There is a very strong sense of his own absence from the beauty of God's creation, and a powerfully imaginative evocation of what those beauties might be, in Matheson's poem, ''The Hidden Beauty'' (II, 1).

He believed it was not just those who were physically blind like himself who needed to use their imaginations to appreciate the full wonder of God's creation. The vision of all mankind was

34

as yet clouded and partial and awaited the evolution of the human soul before it would be made full and perfect. He had a strong sense of the hidden dimension of beauty and wonder in God's creation which would be revealed as human beings progress in sensitivity and perception. It comes over clearly in those meditations which I have grouped together in the section entitled "Now we see through a glass darkly". Here as in other aspects of his theology, it seems to me that Matheson is close to the Eastern Orthodox tradition. He sees human beings as set on a path of deification, gradually moving up towards God and with the eventual prospect of the wonder and splendour of the Divine plan being made manifest on this earth.

It is easy to see how the darkness and isolation brought about by Matheson's blindness could have enhanced his sense of expectancy of a coming time when God and his glory would be revealed to his children in a blaze of light and colour. But it is a measure of the sensitivity and the discipline of his Christian imagination that he did not allow it to turn into mere fantasy and wishful thinking. He had a profound sense of the darker side of God – His hiddenness in clouds and shadows, in lonely and empty places. This theme links the first group of meditations that I have selected below. Once again there are clear echoes here both of his own blindness and also of Eastern Orthodox theology. The idea that God and Christ are to be encountered primarily in the darkness is found in the writings of many of the Greek Fathers. In the early third century Origen developed a highly complex set of images around the idea of Christ as a shadow rather than a light and in the fourth century Gregory of Nyssa portrayed the journey of the Christian soul towards God as an ascent from light to ever greater darkness on the basis of Moses' encounters with the Lord in the cloud on Mount Sinai.

Matheson's meditations on this theme also have some affinity with the notion of the dark night of the soul developed by the sixteenth century Spanish mystic St John of the Cross. He actually likened the Christian faith to blindness since "it informs us of matters we have never seen, or known, either in themselves or in their likeness" and argued that, like the blind, those seeking for closer union with God "must lean on dark faith, accept it as their guide and light and rest on nothing of what they understand, taste, feel or imagine". Through his blindness Matheson had his own dark night of the soul and knew only too well the feelings of desolation that it brought. Yet, like St John of the Cross, he could still frequently and sincerely thank God for the void places in his heart and for the sense of emptiness that he often experienced, believing that human beings were in fact nearer to the Divine presence in this state than when they were full of the joys of life (I, 6).

George Matheson's imaginative faculties were greatly enhanced by his memory. He himself had once beheld the world and its beauties, if only dimly, and the scenes which he remembered from his youth formed an important stock of imagery on which he was to draw in his theological and devotional writings. He had, indeed, achieved that state which William Wordsworth prayed for his sister Dorothy to attain

> When thy mind
> Shall be a mansion for all lovely forms,
> Thy memory be as a dwelling-place
> For all sweet sounds and harmonies

Like that other blind poet who had once enjoyed sight, John Milton, Matheson stored up the memories of sea, cloud and sky, flowers and stars from his youth and idealized them in his writings. I have gathered together some of his meditations on these themes in the section entitled "The World of Nature". Some of them, like his thoughts on the treatment of animals, have a remarkably modern flavour. He had a great feeling for the physical as well as the spiritual – a strongly Incarnational theology which enabled him to see Christ as present in nature as well as in humanity. Undoubtedly his childhood memories of the beauties of nature played a major part in shaping the imagery from the physical world that he so often used in his writings. He himself was fascinated by the extent to which memory fashions perception, perhaps because he had to rely on it so much. It forms the theme of his meditation "In the Light of Eternity" (II, 2) in which he looks forward as well as back and makes the point that to be properly understood the world needs to be seen in the light of its future destiny.

Matheson had a clear perception of what that destiny was – the gathering of all things

together into Christ and the creation of a new
heaven and a new earth of inconceivable beauty
and splendour. He had an even clearer
perception of the engine that was driving the
world towards that destiny – the power of
sacrifice. His thinking is summed up in his poem
"The Divine Plan of Creation" (IV, 1):

> Thou hast, O Lord, a wondrous plan,
> To build a tower to reach the skies;
> Its base is earth, its progress man,
> Its summit sacrifice.

The theme of sacrifice comes up again and again
in Matheson's writings. I have drawn some of
them together in section IV below. He was
undoubtedly influenced by new thinking on this
subject by mid-nineteenth-century theologians.
The old idea of propitiating or satisfying an
angry Deity was giving way to a much deeper
and more compassionate theology where the
principle of sacrifice was seen as lying at the
very heart of the Universe and God himself as
the ultimate exponent of self-giving love,
sacrificing his own Son to give life to mankind.
Matheson himself at one point describes God as
"the Spirit of sacrificial love" (II, 6).

This new theology of sacrifice had been
worked out most fully by the Anglican Christian
Socialist, F. D. Maurice, in a series of sermons
published in 1854 under the title *The Doctrine of
Sacrifice*. I feel sure that Matheson must have
read this work and that it left a deep impression
on him. Maurice argued that far from being a
jealous or angry deity keen to see the punishment

of his faithless creatures, God was rather the author of life through sacrifice and Christ the demonstration of that life. It was through sacrifice that the created world came into existence and through sacrifice that its evils were thwarted. The principle of sacrifice belonged to the very constitution of the Universe. It was not an after-thought introduced by God to deal with an unfortunate situation but a principle that "lies at the very root of our being – our lives stand upon it; society is held together by it".

Matheson strongly adhered to this view of the Atonement. He was particularly fond of preaching on the text from Revelation, 13:8, "The Lamb slain from the foundation of the world", to show how Christ's death had not been an accident but part of God's plan from the beginning. For him, as for Maurice, sacrifice was the animating principle that brought forth new life in both the natural and the supernatural worlds. As he wrote in one of his many sermons on this theme, "All things shine by passing into the life of others: the seed into the flower, the sun into nature, the sea into the reflections of light. Each stage of human life expands by sacrifice of the self-will".

This same theme underlies the closing lines of 'O love that wilt not let me go':

I lay in dust life's glory dead,
And from the ground there blossoms red
    Life that shall endless be.

Explaining this somewhat puzzling imagery, Matheson wrote, "I took red as the symbol of that sacrificial life which blooms by shedding itself''.

It was in terms of the universal principle of sacrifice that he found if not an explanation then at least a purpose for all the world's suffering. One of his parishioners in Edinburgh recalled that one of the commonest themes for his sermons was "The perfection of man through suffering. He shed many a ray of light on the mystery of pain. He taught us that God meant us to overcome the pains of life, not by avoiding them, but by taking them to our hearts and passing them through our souls. We were to conquer all enemies by conquering all our enmity to them. Man was made by God to become perfect through sufferings, not to be made perfectly free from sufferings''. In practical terms this meant not just the acceptance of pain and adversity but also a total surrender of self to God and to fellow human beings. "There are four phases in the birth of the religious life", he began one of his meditations in *Moments on the Mount*, "self-awakening, self-reflection, self-help and self-abandonment". It was only through such self-abandonment that true liberty could be found, that blessed state that comes from following Him whose service is perfect freedom and which Matheson expressed so beautifully in his poem, "Make me a captive, Lord, and then I shall be free" (VI, 3).

The image which Matheson returned to most often to express his ideas of sacrifice and self-abandonment is that of the sea. Perhaps it was because its sound had been the constant accompaniment of his lonely evenings in the manse at Innellan. There is a particularly interesting and highly original meditation which he based on the text of Revelation, 21:1: "And there was no more sea" (IV, 2). This passage is usually interpreted in terms of the Ancient World's dread of the sea and as a promise that at the Second Coming this sign of chaos and evil in the natural world will be no more. But Matheson's rich imagination gives it a wholly new meaning.

Human life below has more sea than land. It is not a connected continent – a brotherhood of souls; it is a multitude of little islands divided by stormy waves. There is a great gulf fixed between my life and the life of my brother – the gulf of self-interest; I cannot pass over to him and he cannot pass over to me . . . . But in that higher life which the seer of Patmos saw the gulfs were all dried up, and the separation of land from land appeared no more. Human nature became to his gaze a continent. Men lost their isolation and ran together in unity . . . . There was perfect self-forgetfulness, therefore there was no more sea.

Many religious traditions have used the image of the sea to express their beliefs about what happens at death. The idea of human souls being carried down like rivers until they merge into the infinity of the ocean is particularly a feature of Hinduism and Buddhism. Matheson paints something of the same picture in the first verse of "O love that wilt not let me go" when he speaks of the individual's life being given back to God "that in thine ocean depths its flow may richer, fuller be". But he parts company with the Eastern religions in wanting to stress the retention of the individual human personality after death, while believing that this is only achieved through the surrender of self-love:

Thou speakest of losing thyself in the ocean of His love, but this is only poetically true. Love is an ocean where no man permanently loses himself; he regains himself in richer, nobler form. The only ocean in which a man loses himself is self-love; God's love gives him back his life that he may keep it unto life eternal' (X, 6).

A conviction that the destiny of all humanity, and indeed of all creation, is to find a final and permanent resting place with God permeates all of Matheson's writings. Some meditations and poems which speak particularly eloquently of this theme will be found in the final section of extracts from his work which I have entitled "Finding Our Rest in God". There are many echoes there of St Augustine's great prayer: "Thou awakest us to delight in Thy praises; for Thou madest us for Thyself, and our hearts are restless until they find their rest in Thee".

Intellectual, poet, mystic, preacher and interpreter of the Word of God, Christian apologist, sensitive pastor and traveller along the way of suffering and sorrow – George Matheson was all of these. But above all, I think, he was a man of faith and imagination. Keen as he was to show the compatibility of Christianity with reason and science, he always insisted that faith must precede knowledge (II, 5). He was not able any more than the rest of us are able to explain or understand the mystery of suffering – why Christ died on the Cross, why he should have been stricken by blindness, why so many innocent souls lead lives of pain and misery. But he approached this mystery in a spirit of utter faith. For him St Paul's remark in 2 Corinthians 5:7, ''We walk by faith and not by sight'' was true in a spiritual as well as in a literal way.

George Matheson's faith was strengthened and deepened by his rich imaginative faculty. I can think of few people whose lives and writings better exemplify the contribution that imagination can make to a full and lively Christian faith. His near-contemporary and fellow Scot, George Macdonald, might have been thinking of the blind divine when he wrote in his essay on *The Imagination: Its Functions and Its Culture* (published in 1867):

In very truth a wise imagination, which is the presence of the spirit of God, is the best guide that man or woman can have; for it is not the things that we see the most clearly that influence us the most powerfully; undefined, yet vivid visions of something beyond, something which eye has not seen nor ear heard, have far more influence than any logical sequences whereby the same things may be demonstrated to the intellect. It is the nature of the thing, not the clearness of its outline, that determines its operation.

For George Matheson, seeing nothing of the world as it is but filled with visions of the world as it might and will be, imagination was the form that faith took in the face of the mystery of existence. It was through the eyes of faith that he saw the world and the God whose sacrificial love through Jesus Christ gives it its very being. And it was with the eyes of imagination that he interpreted the destiny of creation and the point and purpose of human life.

George Matheson's Life

1842	Born in Glasgow
1857	Matriculated as a student of Glasgow University
1861	Graduated with Bachelor of Arts degree
1866	Graduated with Bachelor of Divinity degree Licensed by Presbytery of Glasgow and served probationary year at Trinity Church, Sandyford
1868	Ordained and inducted as minister of Innellan
1874	*Aids to the Study of German Theology*
1877	*The Growth of the Spirit of Christianity*
1881	*Natural Elements of Revealed Theology* "O Love that wilt not let me go" written
1882	*My Aspirations*
1884	*Moments on the Mount*
1885	*Can the Old Faith Live with the New?* Preaches before Queen Victoria at Crathie Church

1886	Inducted as minister of St Bernard's Church, Edinburgh
1887	*The Psalmist and the Scientist*
1888	*Voices of the Spirit* *Landmarks of New Testament Morality*
1889	*Sacred Songs* first published
1890	*The Spiritual Development of St Paul*
1892	*The Distinctive Messages of the Old Religions*
1895	*Searchings in the Silence*
1896	*The Lady Ecclesia* *Words by the Wayside*
1897	*The Bible Definition of Religion* *Sidelights from Patmos*
1899	Retires from parish ministry *Studies of the Portrait of Christ* (Vol. 1)
1900	*Studies of the Portrait of Christ* (Vol. 2)
1901	*Times of Retirement* *The Sceptre without a Sword*
1902	*The Representative Men of the Bible*
1904	*Leaves for Quiet Hours*
1906	*Rests by the River* Died in North Berwick and buried in Glasgow Necropolis

Published posthumously: *The Representative Women of the Bible*

I
In Cloud and Shadow

I In Cloud and Shadow

This opening selection of George Matheson's prayers, poems and meditations reflects a theme to which he came back again and again in his writings and which was obviously closely related to his own blindness. They speak of finding God in the darkness of clouds and shadows and provide a striking contrast to the more conventional portrayal of the Almighty as light.

Matheson himself clearly found God in the darkness of his own blindness and he was attracted by those Biblical texts, particularly in the Old Testament, where the Lord is compared to a cloud or shadow. He found this imagery highly suggestive in a number of different ways. Most obviously it underlined the fact that the Lord was present in the bad times as well as the good. It also sounded a note of universality about the human encounter with the divine. As he puts it in "The Medium of the Spirit": "We do not all meet under the sunbeam, but we all meet under the cloud". The cloud could also be interpreted more positively as the shadow of God's wing, as it is in the poem "The Fire and the Cloud". For Matheson it also hinted at something better to come – he felt with the proverb that "The darkest hour is that before the dawn". This sense of expectancy and promise strongly underlies the last three extracts in this selection.

1. The Dark Things of Life

"He discovereth deep things out of darkness, and bringeth out to light the shadow of death." Job 12:22

My soul, do not despise the shadows of life. Do not say that they are exceptions to the proof of Divine Intelligence; do not exclaim when they are passing over thee that thy way is hid from the Lord. These shadows are sent to thee, not as hidings, but as *revelations* of the face of God; they come to thee as messengers of light. They tell thee what thou couldst not know without them – that there is a life stronger than the natural life. How couldst thou learn that, if the natural life never failed thee? How could faith begin if sight were perfect? How could trust exist if there were no darkness? It is the darkness that lights thee, it is from the shadows that thy spiritual nature is illuminated. From the sense of human emptiness thou reachest that prophetic hunger which is certain to be filled; thy life rises, phoenix-like, from the ashes of thy dying, and out of thy deepest darkness God says, ''Let there be light''.

Moments on the Mount

2. The Medium of the Spirit

"The Lord came down in a cloud, and spake unto him, and took of the Spirit that was upon him, and gave it unto the seventy elders."
Numbers 11:25

God often speaks to me in a cloud – reveals Himself through that which seems an absence of revelation. The hour of sorrow becomes my hour of communion, and the silence of earth is vocal with songs of heaven. But the great advantage of my cloud is that it breaks my solitude. It seems beforehand to be a source of solitude. It threatens to be something which will hide me from the eyes of my brother man and drive me within the temple of my own soul. In reality it has the opposite effect. The message which comes to me through the cloud comes to me as a message for humanity. It first clothes me in the spirit of peace, and then it takes the spirit it has put upon me, and puts it on my fellow-labourers. It enables me to feel that I have one common burden with those who work by my side. It tells me that I am never so little alone, never so near to the mass of mankind, as under the shadow of the night. We do not all meet under the sunbeam, but we all meet under the cloud. The cloud is the true conductor of the electric spark of love. It carries my life into your life, my thought into your thought, my heart into your heart. It finds an entrance through the walls which prosperity has reared between man and man and unites the soul of David to the soul of Jonathan.

Son of Man, let Thy cross be my medium of human brotherhood. Under the shadow of Thy cloud let me meet face to face with the soul of my fellow-man. May we be bound together in the unity of Thy Spirit – the spirit of sacrifice, the spirit of self-surrendering love. May we be united by the fellowship of the mystery – the mystery of suffering. We have failed to be united by the fellowship of prosperity, the participation in a common joy. Join us by Thy cross, O Son of Man; unite us by Thy sacrifice; connect us by Thy cloud. Bring our hearts into sympathy by the contact of a kindred experience, by the touch of a common cross, by the pain of a united martyrdom. Let us walk through the furnace not one by one but three by three and seeing ever the form of a fourth in the likeness of Thyself. It shall be worth while to have met Thee in the cloud if the spirit which Thou there shalt give me shall be the spirit of humanity.

Voices of the Spirit

3. The Fire and the Cloud

"In the day-time also He led them with a cloud, and all the night with a light of fire." Psalm 78:14

Lend me, O Lord, Thy softening cloud
　When sunshine makes a heaven below,
Lest in the desert I be proud,
　Forgetful whence the sunbeams flow!

2 Lend me, O Lord, Thy fire Divine
　When darkness hides Thee from my soul,
Lest in the desert I repine,
　Forgetful whence the shadows roll!

3 Be Thou the shade on my right hand
　When in my strength I stand alone;
And when in night I lose the land,
　Be Thou my star, my guiding One!

4 Cloud of the Cross, Light of the Crown,
　With eve and morn my path beset;
Let pride on Calvary's steep lie down,
　Let faith arise on Olivet!

5 Thy cloud that meets me in the day
　Is but the shadow of Thy wing,
Concealing from my sight the way,
　That faith alone may homeward bring.

6 Thy fire that meets me in the night
　Is the full brightness of Thy face,
Revealing through my tears a light
　That leads me to Thy dwelling-place.

Sacred Songs

4. God's Promise of the Cloud

"The shadow of a great rock in a weary land."
Isaiah 32:3

God is commonly represented as a *light* to the soul; here He is represented as a shadow to the soul. This latter experience is one which we do not often think of. We are quite familiar with prayers for the sunshine. We say constantly, "Rise upon our night, Thou better Sun, and let the clouds melt before Thy glory!' But we are not in the habit of saying, "O Thou Divine Cloud, grant us a moment of Thy Shadow; come and shade us from the glare and glitter of the garish day!' Such a prayer would be deemed very original, perhaps very unsuitable. And yet there are times in which man needs nothing so much as a withdrawal of light. There are times in which the only chance for a human soul is the pulling down of the window-blinds.

We pray, "Enlighten our eyes!" but often we can only get our inner eye enlightened by having the outer eye shaded. Is the soul never to get moments for repose – for meditation, self-reflection! Is it never to have an hour all to itself – an hour when its doors are shut, when its windows are covered, when its outside voices are hushed, when it is untouched by the heat of the day! God says, "Yes, it *shall* have such moments"; and He prepares a place for it in the wilderness. He stops me midway in the race. He lays His hand upon me, and I fall. He bears me into the silence, into the solitude. He puts the multitude all out, and locks the door. He closes the shutters of the casement. He interrupts the music in the street; He forbids the dancing in the hall. He says, "Your nerves are weary with excitement; in this desert place you shall rest awhile."

O Lord my God, have I ever thanked Thee for the shadow; have I ever said with the Psalmist, "The Lord is the shade on my right hand, therefore the sun will not smite me by day, neither the moon by night"! Alas, my Father, mine has been the opposite fear; I am afraid of being smitten by the *absence* of the sun, by the absence of the moon. I have never realized the healing power of the shadow. I have been praying, "Lead, kindly light!' all the time Thou wert giving the command, "Lead, kindly Shade!"

In my day of darkness Thy light broke. I never knew my immortality till, behind the curtains drawn, I felt my sin. It was the *shadow* taught me immortality. The sunshine said, "The building is complete; why look for a tomorrow!" But the shadow said, "You are unfinished; there is a tower wanting; there is something to come." The sunshine cried, "You are satisfied on earth; earth is your portion." But the shadow murmured, "Your powers are unfilled here; you wait a wider field". The sunshine sang, "This is the day the Lord hath made". But the shadow whispered "The end is not yet; there remaineth a rest to the people of God". Thy shadow, O Lord, has been better than man's light.

Rests by the River

5. The Shadow of God

"The children of men put their trust under the shadow of Thy wings" Psalm 36:7

There is a shadow that calms our cares,
  There is a curtain that brings us light,
There is a cloud that the Father wears
  When His love is too strong for sight;
When the fire of His presence draws too near
  He brings me down to the valley's shade,
And His glory is hid from eye and ear
  In the cloud that His love has made.

2 I thought at first when my sorrow came
  It proved that my Father was far away,
And in all the world there was no name
  To whom my soul could pray;
But when, ere ever the cloud passed by,
  I felt a strength in the midst of gloom,
I knew that my Father must be nigh,
  And my heart burst into bloom.

3 I have reared in shadow my flower of love,
  It has bloomed, O Father, by night to Thee;
It has opened its petals to hopes above,
  To a day it could not see;
And in time to come I shall fear no foe,
  Though the sky be dark and the air be chill,
For I know that the flower of love can glow
  When the sun has set on the hill.

Sacred Songs

6.   The Unexpected Door of Revelation

"A voice came out of the cloud" Mark 9:7

If you had been standing on the Mount of Transfiguration you would have said, "Here at last I shall have a revelation from the silent heaven." You would have felt in looking round that there was hardly a single door through which that revelation might not come. You would have expected it from the glittering garments. You would have looked for it from the shining face. You would have anticipated it from the two celestial visitors. You would have been prepared to receive it from the audible words of communion between the two worlds. You would have said, "There is only one little corner where I expect a shut door; I see a tiny cloud covering a bit of the blue." Now, what is the real state of the case? In the whole of that mountain scene there was only one object which became the avenue for revelation – it was the tiny cloud! None of the likely things became a medium. The white garments said nothing. The shining countenance revealed nothing.The celestial visitors brought nothing. The converse of heaven and earth explained nothing. But the cloud – the despised cloud – the rejected cloud – the cloud that seemed to throw a damper on the scene – that was the thing which spoke, that was the thing which revealed the glory of the Son of Man! Nobody would now deny that it is the cloud which has revealed Christ's glory; our watchword is not the shining of His countenance, but the shadow of His Cross. Yet not of Christ alone has the symbol proved true; the voice to you and me has come from the cloud. What reveals our higher birth? Is it the shining garment of our mountain moments – the triumphs of reason, the discoveries of science, the achievements of art, the advances of music? Not these. Is it the increase in the power of human converse – the marvels of steam and electricity? Not these. Is it the possession of tabernacles of gold – the trappings of wealth, the homes of luxury, the gardens of pleasure? Not these. It is our cloud that reveals our origin. It is our wants that prove our birth. It is our thirst that betrays our aristocracy. It is the rent in our garment that shows how we in the body are not at home. We have torn our garb because it is too small for us; our cloud has made our parentage clear.

I thank Thee, O Lord, for the void places in my heart; they reveal more than does the furniture. I see Thee nearest where I am not filled; it is the *empty* air that gives me wings. All my treasures have come from the shadow. My faith needs the fog. My prayer needs the precipice. My trust needs the tempest. My sympathy needs the sacrifice. My mercy needs the miserable. My truth needs temptation. My pity needs painfulness. My peace needs powers opposing. My spotlessness needs contact with a stain. How could I hope if there were no haze! – hope would be lost in certainty. How could I be patient if there were no perils! – patience would melt in fruition. How could I be charitable if there were no cheerless! – charity would fade in wastefulness. How could I feel immortal if there were no insufficiency! – earth would be then my fitting rest. It is on the wings of weakness I fly to Thee. It is in the days of darkness I cry to Thee. It is in the sense of sinfulness I sigh to Thee. My gem lies in my conscious degeneracy; I discern my origin when I recognize the dust. The ring and the robe may welcome me back, the music and the dancing may greet my return; but it is the famine that tells me I am wandered, it is the sense of the swine-husks that brings me home.

Rests by the River

II
Now We See Through a Glass Darkly

II Now We See Through a Glass Darkly

One of the effects of George Matheson's blindness was to heighten his sense that in this world we only glimpse a tiny part of the glory that is one day going to be revealed to us. He had a great sense of the beauty that lay hidden not just from those like himself who were without the use of their eyes but from all of us because of our spiritual imperfection and blindness. This theme is vividly explored in his poem, ''The Hidden Beauty'' and it lies behind all the writings in this section.

Matheson felt strongly that it is only in the light of God's ultimate plan and our eternal destiny that the present world, with its joys as well as its sorrows, will be explained and made clear. This is the central message of his meditations ''In the Light of Eternity'' and ''How to Search for Truth''. All that we can do here and now is to make the leap of faith that must precede knowledge (''Faith and Knowledge''), let our imaginataion soar up to the hills rather than keeping our eyes cast down on the prosaic plains (''The Beginnings of Salvation'') and follow the orbitless star (''Man's Premonition of Christmas Bells'').

1. The Hidden Beauty

"The earnest expectation of the creation waiteth for the manifestation of the sons of God" Romans 8:19

Lord, Thou hast spread o'er earth and sea
A beauty yet unknown to me,
   All buried from my view;
I have not seen one half the charms
That nature folds within her arms,
   Ancient but ever new.

2 Creation doth not yet command
A meed of justice from my hand
   For all that Thou hast given;
If I had but another sense,
Her beauties would be so intense
   That earth would be my heaven.

3 I do not need to soar above
To find in dwellings of Thy love
   A lovelier scene than earth;
One dormant lens revived to power
Would kindle tints in every flower
   That would renew my birth.

4 Creation waits as ages roll,
Expectant of the perfect soul
   To look upon her face –
Expectant of the glorious day
When man with powers of larger ray
   Shall see Thy hidden grace.

5 Thou keepest for the coming eye
  A thousand colours in the sky
    Unpainted in my dream;
  Thou keepest for the future ear
  A thousand notes of music clear
    That now all-voiceless seem.

6 'Tis not in change of earth or air
  I seek a paradise more rare,
    More beautiful to see;
'Tis only by my widening mind
  I hope a fairer world to find –
    Increased in wealth to me.

7 Before my soul Thy beauty waits,
  And entrance seeks at fastened gates
    That no response return;
  Thy flowers are left beside each door,
  And there they lie the long year o'er
    For every foot to spurn.

8 But when my doors shall open wide,
  I shall behold a sight outside
    That shall inspire my praise;
  For, in the meanest forms below,
  The light of all Thy worlds shall glow
    With ever-varied rays.

9 Praise waits for Thee in nature, Lord;
  It waits till human life has soared
    To its appointed height,
  When Thou shalt end Thy work in man,
  Then only shall we hail the plan
    That said, "Let there be light!"

Sacred songs

2. In the Light of Eternity

"In thy light shall we see light" Psalm 36:9
"The lamb is the light thereof" Revelation 21:23

Nothing is seen in its own light – not even a visible thing. A landscape is not seen in its own light; it is perceived very much in the light of yesterday. How little of what you see is mere perception! Every sight of nature is tinged with the light of memory. The poet looks from the bridge at midnight upon the rushing waters; but what he sees is not the flowing tide, it is a tide of *memory* which fills his eyes with tears. You listen to the babbling of the brook; but what you hear is not the babbling, it is the utterance of a dear name. You visit Rome, you visit Jerusalem, you visit Greece; do you see any of these by its own light? No; they are all beheld by the light of yesterday; *there* is their glory, there lies their gold! "Even so," cries the Psalmist, "it is with this world; if you want *to* see it, you must look at it by the light of another world – God's *coming* world. He does not mean that when we quit the scenes of earth we shall have a bright light in heaven. It is more than that. It is for the scenes of earth he wants the heavenly light. He says you cannot interpret your own skies without it. We often say that in the light of eternity earthly objects will fade from our sight. But the Psalmist says that until we get the light of eternity earthly objects will not be *in* our sight. It is by the light of the Celestial City – the City which has no need of the sun – that alone

we can tell what here is large and what here
is small.

Thou Lamb, slain from the foundation of the
world, Thou art the Light thereof! When God
said, "Let us make man!" He meant not Adam,
but Thee. Thou art the plan of the great building;
to Thee all things move. By no other light can
I understand the struggles of this earth. Not by
nature's light can I understand them; I have seen
the physical sunshine sparkle on my pain, and
I thought it a cruel thing. Not by philosophy's
light can I understand them; I have seen the
great thinker impeded by poverty and I thought
it an unseemly thing. Not in beauty's light can
I understand them; I have seen the artist lose
his eyesight and I thought it an unrighteous
thing. But if the world is being woven for *Thee*,
I understand. If Thy type of sacrifice is the plan
of the Architect, I understand. If Thy cross is
Creation's crown, I understand. If the Celestial
City is a home for hospital training, I understand.
If Thine angels are all ministering spirits, I
understand. If the purest robe is not the white
robe but the robe *washed* white, if the goal of
man is not Eden but Gethsemane, if the glory
of Thy Father is the sacrificial blood of love, then
have I found the golden key, in Thy Light I have
seen Light!

Leaves for Quiet Hours

3. The Beginnings of Salvation

"How beautiful upon the mountains are the feet of Him that bringeth good things!" Isaiah 52:7

Christ in the soul descends from the mountain to the valley. Divine knowledge follows the opposite course to human knowledge. Human knowledge rises from earth to heaven; the boy learns geography before he studies astronomy. But Divine knowledge descends from heaven to earth. Its first influence is exerted on the high places, the places nearest the sky. The feet of Christ are first seen on the mountains. The beginning of the Divine life is high aspiration. You have seen the tops of the hills aflame with morning gold while the plain and the valley were in shadow. Even so is it with the life of the soul.

If you want to know a man's spiritual prospects, it is to the *hills* you must lift up your eyes. You must judge his morning hours not by what he does but by what he thinks. You must measure him by his aspirations. You must seek the feet of the coming Lord, not in the man's deeds, but in his *desires* to do. That is why at the beginning we are said to be justified, not by works, but by faith. It is a great kindness in our Father to make the test of us, not what we do, but what we dream of. In the absence of our good actions our Father will impute to us our good dreams. He will accept Christ's footprints while as yet they are only on the mountains.

And that is my comfort, O my Father. My deeds are far behind. Neither on the plain nor in the valley do I yet reveal Thy footprints. But the mountains are already in a glow. I have *dreams* of Thy Christ, aspirings after His beauty, longings for His love. Though not yet do I follow Him, He stands upon my highest hill. He is the climax of my hopes, the acme of my wishes, the height of my ambitions, the ideal of what I should *like* to be. On the mountain of my heart. His feet are already beautiful. Keep Thine eye upon the mountain, O my Father! Behold my dreams of Him, my dreams of Thee! Look not yet on my plain! Gaze not yet on my valley! Expect not yet the footprints of Thy Christ on the beaten path! My walk is still imperfect, but I have learned to soar. Judge me by my soaring! Receive me by the rising of my wing! Accept my *cry* for Thy Christ! Open Thy gates to my *dreams* of Thee! Unbar Thy heavens to the mere sigh of my spirit! Meet me on the mountain – on the places paved as yet only with my good intentions! Come to me with the ring and the robe and the welcome while for Thee I have only the resolve, "I will arise and go to my Father"! Behold in that desire the feet of Thy Christ upon the hill!

Rests by the River

4. Man's Premonition of Christmas Bells

"We have seen His star." Matthew 2:2

The star was a thing for which Nature had no use. It served no physical purpose. It was superfluous so far as secular need is concerned; there was no place for it in the merely natural sky. That is the reason the wise men believed it to be *super*natural. Its light gave no help to the present world; they said, "It must have a function in some other world." And this is precisely how we reason in our moments of premonition. We see something very beautiful for which we can find no earthly purpose; and we say, "It must have a purpose elsewhere; we have seen the light of an undawned day." What, for example, is the mundane use of poetry! Does it help the development of the world! To the business man it is rather a hindrance; it tends to make him unpractical. To the schoolboy it is a retardation; it makes him dream when he should be studying; you cannot see the beauties of "Paradise Lost" at the same time that you are parsing it. To the dispenser of charity it is a barrier – real sorrow seems so prosaic compared with ideal sorrow. Whence then has it come – seeing that earthly need has not created it! It is not an evolution; it is a premonition. For any time-purpose it might be called a useless organ; but its use is coming. It tells us that we are preparing for something ideal – for a Christ who is "fairer than the children of men," for an "Altogether Lovely," for a presence "without blemish and

70

without spot"; in poetry "we have seen His star."

I thank thee, O Lord, that there are things in this world which this world does not need. I thank Thee that there are things called unpractical – unusable. It is from these I get my hope; they are my "star". Other things give me earthly riches – the gold and the frankincense and the myrrh; but the star gives me my Christ. My finest treasures are in this world bound in a napkin. My dreams disqualify me, my star-gazing strands me. I seem to be only on the road to a manger – a place where inferior intelligences dwell. So I am, if this world were all. Why hast Thou suffered the boy to see castles in the fire when he ought to be studying his map? Why hast Thou permitted the youth to see stars above his ledger when he ought to be studying his figures? Why hast Thou allowed the maiden to dream of romantic beauties which domestic life will never yield? Why hast Thou caused Matthew to forget the count of his tax-gathering in a vision of loveliness? Why hast Thou made Peter drop his fishing-rod for a call that could bring no bread? Why hast Thou sent Nicodemus a night dream that makes him less successful with the world by day? Oh! it is all the star – the star of Bethlehem! It is because in the great world to which I go these powers disused of earth will be all the vogue. It is to ripen me for *Thy* riches, to train me for *Thy* treasures, to fit me for *Thy* fulness, to leaven me for *Thy* light. I thank Thee, O Lord, that, amidst the many constellations whose path I can trace, there is revealed to me at moments one orbitless star.

Rests by the River

5. Faith and Knowledge

"And we believe and are sure that Thou art that Christ, the Son of the living God." John 6:69

"We believe and are sure;" more strictly it should be rendered, "We *have* believed and are sure." The thought of the apostle is that there has been a development in his experience; he began by simple faith, and he has ended with assured knowledge. Such is ever the order of the Christian understanding; we first believe, and then we know. Faith is not the opposite of knowledge; it is the anticipation, the prophecy of knowledge. Faith is to knowledge what the swallow is to the summer – the messenger that sings its coming. Faith soars up to heaven in the morning and sees in advance the plan of the unfolding day. It cannot yet trace the plan, it cannot yet tell how the plan is to *be* unfolded, but it beholds what it cannot analyse, it trusts what it cannot verify.

So was it with the Master when He first said to His disciples, "Follow me." Why should He have hoped that they would follow Him? They did not yet know Him. But He felt that they must follow Him before they knew Him, that they could only come to know Him through the experience of being near Him. And so He called upon another faculty than knowledge; He appealed to the power of their faith. He said, Give me the prophetic trust of your souls. I am come to lead you by the green pastures and beside the quiet waters, to let you know by the walk of experience that the pastures of life *are* green, and that the waters of life *are* quiet. But you can only come to know it by *walking* with me. You must come to me without knowledge, without proof, without experience; you must give me your faith. Pay me with your love *in advance*. I do not ask it without return; I will repay its value tenfold – in work, in sacrifice, but I cannot work *for* you unless you will first let me work *through* you. Grant me your sympathy beforehand. Grant me the mesmeric look of faith, that I may fill your life with my presence. Grant me the steadfast gaze of the eye, that I may transform you into my own image. Grant me the complete surrender of the will, that I may make your will my will. When I have made your will my will there shall be no more room for faith; faith shall be lost in sight, and ye shall know as ye are known. Trust me but one hour with the treasure of your hearts, and with rich interest I will give them back to you again; lend them to me with faith, and I will restore them to you with knowledge – that knowledge of me which is life eternal. In that hour you shall be able to say, "Once we believed, now we are sure."

Moments on the Mount

6. How to Search for Truth

"God is light." 1 John 1:5

Light; what is it? It is not something to search for; it is something to search *by*. No man by searching can find out God; but, if he take God without searching, he will find everything else. My evidence for God is what He shews me. I must have a torch to begin with. The room is dark and I have lost something – the key to my own nature. I cannot find it till I have struck a light. There must be light in my hand before I come in – light on the threshold, light at the very door. My progress must not be from the dark into the clear but from the clear into the dark. God is His own interpreter; in God's light shall we see light.

My Father, come to me in life's dawn. Help me to find the lost key. All things without Thee are mystery, nay, they are impossible; how shall they prove *Thee* when Thou art needed to prove *them?* The manger will not lead me to the star; but the star can lead me to the manger. If Thou art love, then, Thy best gift must be sacrifice; in that light let me search Thy world. It has pains wrapt up in every pleasure, and who shall explain them? Only Thyself – the Spirit of sacrificial love. We make all things in our own image, and Thou hast made the world in Thine. It is not faultlessly fair; but its spots are from the plan of the Artist. Let me see the Artist ere I gaze on the picture. Be Thou Thyself my light into every darkness.

Searchings in the Silence

III
The World of Nature

III *The World of Nature*

George Matheson strikes an extraordinarily modern note in his references to the world of nature and his advocacy of animal rights. The starting point for his meditations on "Kindness to Animals" and "The Spirit of the Animal World" is the fact that humans are in fellowship with all other creatures, or, as he puts it, "that you and they together are the offspring of God". In his poem, "The Common Want", all of nature, from the birds in the upland to the wide forests, is portrayed as being united in praying, crying, waiting, sighing and weeping for God in a way that recalls St Paul's graphic description in Romans 8:22 of the whole creation "groaning in travail together".

The importance of the physical, earthly element in the Christian faith is the subject of the last three meditations in this section which speak powerfully of the Incarnation and its consequence that Christ is to be found in the flower as much as in the tract and that he is recognized as Lord and Saviour by the wayward elements of wind and wave as well as by human disciples.

1. Kindness to Animals

"And God said, Let us make man in our image, and let them have dominion over the fish of the sea, and over the fowl of the air, and over the cattle." Genesis 1:26

God never gives dominion to any creature which has not reached His image. His image is love. Other things *belong* to God; but God *is* love. No creature that has not love will be allowed to have a permanent empire. The Father of Mercy will not put the reins of government into a hand that has no heart. Dominion is a very solemn thing; it may oppress, crush, destroy. The Father must have a guarantee for its gentleness. What guarantee can there be but His own image – the possession of a nature tender as the Divine? Ye who torture the beast of the field, have you considered the ground of your authority? Have you pondered why it is that God has given you the dominion? It is because He meant you to have His image ere you began to reign. If you have not a tender heart, you have no right to reign; you are a usurper. Is it not written that Christ Himself has authority to exercise judgment because He is the Son of *Man* – because He has a soul of infinite tenderness? Shall the disciple be above his Lord? If you would reign with Him, you must first suffer with Him – feel the pains of sympathy for the wants below. It is the meek who shall inherit the earth; God's dominion is for God's love.

My Father, fill me with love for things beneath me. Forbid that I should be cruel to the beast of the field. Give me the tenderness that is born of reverence. Teach me to revere the creation that is under me. Was not its life a stream from Thy life? Is not its life a mystery to me even now? Does it not accomplish without reasoning what I cannot do *by* reasoning? Let me uncover my head before the mystery. Shall I bruise that which is so full of Thee, which surpasses me even while it obeys me? I think I can understand why men of old worshipped the animal. It was the sense of an avenue of knowledge beyond all human avenues – that there are more modes of Thy inspiration than we dream of in our philosophies. Let me take up tenderly that which I do know. There are wants in beast and bird which to me are no mysteries, for they are my own. Give me fellowship with these, oh, my Father. Let me enter into sympathy with their hunger, their thirst, their weariness, their cold, their frequent homelessness. Let me give their wants a place in my prayers. Let me remember them in the struggles of the forest. Let me remember them in the neglect of the city. Let me remember them in the winter's frost and snow. Let me be to them what Thou hast been to me – a protector, a Providence. I shall be worthy to have Thy dominion when I have reached Thy image.

Searchings in the Silence

2. The Spirit in the Animal World

"These wait all upon Thee . . . Thou sendest forth Thy Spirit, they are created." Psalm 104:27, 30

Who are the "all" here spoken of? They are the living creatures of the whole earth. What! you say, the creatures of the animal world! can *these* be said to be in possession of God's Spirit? I can understand very well how *man* should be thus privileged. I can understand why a being of such nobleness as the human soul should lay claim to a distinctive pre-eminence. But is it not a bold thing to say that the human soul is in contact with the beast of the field? Is it not a degradation of my nature to affirm that the same Spirit which created me created also the tenants of the deep? No, my brother; if you shall find in God's Spirit the missing link between yourself and the animal world you will reach a Darwinism where there is nothing to degrade. You are not come from them, but you and they together are the offspring of God. Would you have preferred to have had no such link between you?

It is your forgetfulness of that link that has made you cruel to the creatures below. You do not oppress your brother man, because you know him to be your brother; but you think the beast of the field has no contact with the sympathy of your soul. It *has* a contact, an irrefragable, indestructible contact. You are bound together by one Spirit of creation; you sit at one communion table of nature; you are members of one body of natural life. The glory of being united to thy Father is that in Him thou shalt be united to everything. Thou shalt be allied not only to the highest but to the lowest, thou shalt be able not only to go up but to go down. Thou shalt have the power that thy Lord had – the power to empty thyself to the lowermost, to the uttermost. Thou shalt feel that thou owest all things thy sympathy when thou hast recognized this relationship through the same divine Spirit.

Voices of the Spirit

3. The Common Want

"The eyes of all wait upon Thee; and Thou givest them their meat in due season." Psalm 145:15

They are all praying, praying,
  Breathing their wants to Thee;
Birds in the uplands straying,
  Lives of the land and sea,
Songs at the heavenly portals,
  Wails in the forest wide,
Sighs from the heart of mortals
  Weary of pomp and pride.

2 They are all crying, crying,
  Bound by a kindred tie,
Bound by the fetters lying
  Down where all instincts lie –
Bound by a want impelling
  Each higher up the shore,
Linked in a common dwelling
  By the same need for more.

3 They are all waiting, waiting
  For Thy great hand to pour
Its treasures unabating
  On air and sea and shore.
But my heart has waited longest,
  And has not found her rest
Where the sparrow's house is strongest
  And most sure the swallow's nest.

4 But through my sighing, sighing,
   I can read Thy promise true;
My fruits Thou art denying
   Till my season shall be due.
The swallow finds her summer
   In the gateway of the year;
I am a later comer,
   And my fulness is not here.

5 Only, while weeping, weeping
   For the seeds beneath the sight,
Let me feel that Thou art keeping
   These in Thy hidden light!
Let me feel that Thou art warming
   Their growth beneath the ground,
And that harvest life is forming
   For the trumpet's joyful sound!

Sacred Songs

4. The Ministration of the Physical to Faith

"Beautiful for situation is Mount Zion." Psalm 48:2

I do not know in the whole Bible a passage exactly like this. It is the only passage within my memory in which the Bible makes a direct appeal to the sense of physical beauty for its own sake. Generally, Nature is viewed only as the vehicle of *God;* here, it stands for itself and is accorded an independent place as a religious educator. At first, indeed, such words in Scripture sound like an anti-climax. Mount Zion was full of the holiest associations – of memories that were sacramental, of influences that inspired the breath of heaven. Does it not seem a strange thing that amid these sacred qualifications there should be introduced a fact so earthly, so mundane, so physical. "Beautiful for situation." Fancy a preacher inviting one to worship in a particular house of God for such a reason as that!

And yet the psalmist is right. The presence of physical beauty helps worship. All emotion is quickened by environment. Even creative imagination is. The poet may construct a new world; but he will do it better under the stars of heaven than under the roof of a garret. It is easier to be good in a garden than in a hovel. It is easier to love God on the mountain peak than amid the dens of human poverty. It is easier to think of heaven where myriad voices roll their music than where the sounds of wrangling greet the ear.

Why do you bring a flower to the hospital? If you want to teach resignation to an invalid, would not the text or the tract be a better medium than the painted garniture that meets the eye? No; for you can only teach resignation by entering the mind at a side door – by directing the thought to something else. A man accepts his pain, not by reflecting on it, but by reflecting on other things. The tract bids me be patient; the flower bids me forget. The tract suggests lying down; the flower prophesies springing up. The tract reminds me of my impotence; the flower reveals the glory of lesser things than I. The tract speaks of God's supernatural will; the flower tells of God's supernatural love. The tract says, "Look into your heart and be humble"; the flower cries, "Look out on the fields and be glad."

5. The Empire of Jesus

"The men marvelled, saying, What manner of man is this, that even the winds and the sea obey Him!" Matthew 8:27

The marvellous thing about Christ's influence is the nature of the things which He influenced. The winds and the sea – these are the wayward forces, the types of variableness, the elements which cannot be counted on. If one can rule these he must have the root of empire in him. Our marvel at the sway of Jesus is the same marvel as that of the men on the Lake of Galilee – that "the winds and the sea" should obey Him. It is not the number of His followers that startles us. Buddha had more followers; Mohammed had more followers. It is the *quality* of the followers of Jesus that wakes our wonder. They are drawn from "the winds and the sea" – from the sphere of wayward forces.

Both Buddha and Mohammed dwelt in a stagnant atmosphere. They stood, not by the brink of the sea, but by the side of a dead pool. They heard no sound of waves, they listened to no murmur of the storm; theirs was a rod of empire over minds only half awake. But the mission of Jesus was a mission by the sea. His was a message delivered in front of the winds. He spoke to minds which were already on the wing – instinct with new life and separate life. Europe had come over into Asia, and the pulse of Asia had been quickened. Men had ceased to be uniform; they had begun to think independently. Opposite tastes had risen; opposing schools were rising.

And yet this complex world agreed on *Jesus*. He took representatives from every school. He conquered men amid their varieties. He did not first ask them to give up their varieties. He took them into the ark as they were – of every kind. He did not ask them to be of one nature. He let them keep their separate tastes, their different likings. He allowed the winds to blow as before, the sea to wave as before. He required but one article of agreement – obedience to Himself. No wonder the men of Galilee marvelled!

O Lord Jesus Christ, Thine has been the empire of the *West* – an empire over the winds and the sea! Other masters have ruled the Eastern mind; they have wielded the sceptre over sleeping souls and passionless hearts. But Thou hast reigned where passion reigns. Thy flag has waved amid the tempests of the spirit. Thou hast been most adored just where the pulses of life beat strongest. Thine is not the sway over a bruised and broken humanity. Thine is not the dominion over a valley and shadow of death. Thy kingdom has not only the power but the glory. Thy subjects are free souls, living hearts. Thou art king, not where Buddha is king – amid the tombstones, not where Mohammed is king – amid the grave-clothes, but where the streams flow, where the rivers run, where the torrents sweep, where the breezes dance and play. Thy people are *willing* in the day of Thy power; the winds and the sea obey Thee.

Rests by the River

6. The Spiritual in the Earthly

"Supposing Him to be the gardener." John 20:15

We often mistake Christ for the gardener —
attribute to mere physical beauty what comes
from faith alone. We speak of the glories of
Nature; most of its glories belong to man. We
find a sense of infinitude in the breath of the
new-mown hay; yet, truly, it is not in that, but
in *thee*. It has been said: "Thou weavest for God
the garment by which thou seest Him"; more
justly might the words be spoken of Nature. Her
song is the echo of thy song. She answers in
refrain to thee — to thy sorrows and to thy joys.
Often have men exhorted thee to follow the
teachings of Nature, and to look on the things
beyond as an idle dream. Nay, but thy vision of
Nature depends on thy vision of grace.

In vain shalt thou seek in the flower the grace
which is not in thy soul. It is from the things
beyond the earth that earthly beauty flows. The
voice which thou hearest in the garden is the
voice of the Lord. That which uplifts thee in the
flower is just what the gardener has not planted.
It is the life below the stem, the mystery beneath
the root. It is the sense of a presence which has
escaped the eye, of a power which has eluded
the botanist. It is the feeling that the gardener
has planted something which he has not seen —
a seed from the life eternal, a blossom from the
breast of God.

Oh, Thou, whose Easter morning shines in many disguises, help me to recognize Thee everywhere. Let me not ascribe to the gardener the work that is done by Thee. I often speak of the noble lives led by men who do not know Thee; teach me that Thou knowest *them*. Tell me that Thy presence is wider than our creed, Thy temple bigger than our sanctuary, Thy love larger than our law. Convince me that Thou enfoldest that which does not enfold *Thee*. Let me learn that Thou art the one "excellent name in all the earth". Men call their excellent things by other names; they take Thee to be the gardener. Hasten the time when they shall take the gardener to be Thee; they shall be nearer to the truth of things. Hasten the time when "in the flesh they shall see God" – see Him in the forms of earth, see Him in the duties of the hour, see Him in the paths of life, see Him in the progress of the day. Make Thyself known to them in the breaking of the earthly bread; in the planting of the earthly flower let them gaze on *Thee*.

Searchings in the Silence

IV
The Spirit of Sacrifice

IV   The Spirit of Sacrifice

The powerful poem that begins this section
expresses very clearly George Matheson's
conviction that at the very heart of God's plan
for the world lay the principle of sacrifice. The
reason why all life was founded on sacrifice –
why the Lamb was slain from the foundation of
the world – remained a mystery, but it was
clearly attested both by the Christian notion of
atonement and by the observations of scientists
about how progress was made through
evolution.

For Matheson the principle of sacrifice
translated itself in terms of practical Christianity
into a call for selflessness. The loss of selfishness
is explored with rare sensitivity and imagination
in the meditations on "No more sea" and
"Christ's first note of autobiography".

1. The Divine Plan of Creation

"The Lamb slain from the foundation of the world." Revelation 13:8

Thou hast, O Lord, a wondrous plan,
    To build a tower to reach the skies;
Its base is earth, its progress man,
    Its summit sacrifice.

2 'Tis only for the summit's sake
    Thou layest the foundation-stone;
The mornings of creation break
    For sacrifice alone.

3 Thou wouldst not have prepared one star
    To float upon the azure main,
Hadst Thou not witnessed from afar
    The Lamb that would be slain.

4 Thou wouldst not have infused Thy life
    Into the insect of an hour,
Hadst Thou not seen 'neath nature's strife
    Thy sacrificial flower.

5 To Him that wears the cross of pain
    Thou leadest all Thine ages on;
Through cloud and storm, through wind and
      rain,
    Through sense of glories gone.

6 Through kingdoms lost, through pride
      displaced
    Through systems tried and cast away,

Through hopes dispelled, through stars
    effaced,
  Thou leadest to the day.

7 Thou breakest on the rocks of life
    The wills of men that sought their own;
  They sank before Thee in the strife,
    And cried, "Unveil Thy throne!"

8 And in that blest unveiling, Lord,
    They found, I find, the reason sure
  Why Thou hast sent on earth a sword
    From out Thy meekness pure.

9 Thou wilt not let me live alone;
    Thou wilt not let me keep my rest;
  Thy blast on every tree has blown
    To throw me on Thy breast.

10 Thou madest me for Him whose love
    From dawn to eve made His will Thine,
  And all my ages only move
    Within that Light to shine.

Sacred Songs

2. No More Sea

"There was no more sea." Revelation 21:1

Human life below has more sea than land. It is not a connected continent – a brotherhood of souls; it is a multitude of little islands divided by stormy waves. There is a great gulf fixed between my life and the life of my brother – the gulf of self-interest; I cannot pass over to him, and he cannot pass over to me. And the secret of our separation is the secret also of our unrest. We live in perpetual storms because we live in perpetual selfishness; the wave of our thoughts rolls back upon ourselves. But in that higher life which the seer of Patmos saw the gulfs were all dried up, and the separation of land from land appeared no more. Human nature became to his gaze a continent. Men lost their isolation and ran together into unity. They saw eye to eye, they felt heart to heart, they wrought hand to hand, and the glory of the Lord was revealed because all flesh could see it together. Each man took up the trouble of his brother-man, and in taking the trouble of his brother each man lost his own. There came a great stillness over the individual heart. Its stillness came because its burden fell, and its burden fell because the burdens of humanity rose; there was perfect self-forgetfulness, therefore there was no more sea.

O thou Son of Man, who, by lifting the burdens of our humanity, hast made Thine own yoke easy and Thine own burden light, lift this life of mine into sympathy, into union with Thee. I am weary of myself, weary of the din and the battle, weary of the burden and the heat. I am seeking everywhere for a hiding-place from the storm, everywhere for a covert from the tempest. But the storm is not without me, but within; the tempest is not in my circumstances but in me. Son of Man, save me from myself, that I may enter into Thy peace, Thine unspeakable joy. Inspire me with Thine own burden of love, that the care of self may fall from me, and that with Thy divine freedom I may be free. Help me to take up Thy cross, that I myself may be lifted up. Give me Thy spirit of sacrifice, that I may be elevated above my own fears. Unite me to the great continent, the brotherhood of human souls, that the storms of my island life may be lulled to rest; then shall I be able in my heart to say "There is no more sea".

Moments on the Mount

3. Christ's First Note of Autobiography

"Blessed are the poor in spirit." Matthew 5:3

There is a question I have often asked myself – Why does St Matthew bring the Sermon on the Mount so close to the temptation in the wilderness? That is not its natural position; it belongs to a much later stage of Christ's ministry, and could not have been understood in the earliest period. Why, then, does the First Gospel place it in the immediately succeeding chapter to the temptation? I take the reason to be that the first note of this sermon is a reminiscence of our Lord's experience in the wilderness – in other words, it is a note of autobiography.

What was the temptation in the wilderness? I would sum it up in four words – "Be conscious of yourself." The tempter said, "If you are the Son of God, realize that you are such. Let the thought be ever present to your mind. Let your every action be prompted by the motive of showing that you are Divine. Assert yourself in the world. Command that the stones be made bread. Claim the Father's care in a gigantic leap from the pinnacle of the temple. Aspire to the conquest of the kingdoms of the world and the glory of them."

The one thought in all the temptations is the grandeur of self-consciousness. And this is the thought which in the Sermon on the Mount Christ begins by repudiating. It shows what an adverse impression it had made upon His mind. He starts this great sermon by a note of memory

– a memory of His own pain. He remembers how bitterly he felt this perversion of the truth. He is determined it shall be the first delusion He will publicly expose, the first error of which He will warn the multitude. Accordingly, He stands in the midst of them and, with an air of almost dramatic abruptness, cries, "Blessed are the poor in spirit, for theirs is the kingdom of heaven!"

Read that in the light of the wilderness, and it means this – "The highest power, even heavenly power, comes in moments of unconsciousness." To be poor in spirit is to be unconscious of yourself. It is not "to be humble," "to be despondent," "to be miserable" – these are all forms of consciousness. It is to forget that you have an eye or ear, a hand or foot, a heart or brain. It is to fly without hearing the movement of your own wings. It is to ignore the flower you wear, to forget the charm you bear, to discount the deed you dare – to see not when you shine, to feel not it is fine, to say not, "Wealth is mine." That is the spirit whose poverty is power.

Lord, only in Thine unconsciousness shall I reach Thy Mount; let me resist the tempter with *Thee!* My wilderness is my consciousness. I say, "If I leap from the pinnacle, I shall prove my trust in God" – and very likely my courage will fail. But if a *friend* fall from the pinnacle, I make an *un*conscious leap – the leap of self-forgetfulness. The world marvels at my courage. It is the want of courage. Love's fear has

101

paralysed me, made me oblivious of myself. Give me, O Christ, that fear which makes oblivious! – it was *Thine*. It is not courage that makes us unconscious of peril; it is the fear that is born of love.

Men exhort me to have the fear of the Lord. They are right. Thy fear is love's fear – the only fear which deadens personal pain. It makes heroes of the helpless, warriors of the weak, soldiers of the sick, lions of the listless, Daniels of the drooping, fortresses of the feeble, champions of little children, youth's morning light of the fulness of years. Lord of the beatitudes, grant me this boon!

Rests by the River

V
The Christian Life

V The Christian Life

As a liberal Presbyterian minister, George Matheson was concerned with preaching practical Christianity and expounding the social gospel just as much as with pondering more abstract theological questions and with prayer and devotion. The meditations in this section are about living the Christian life. They have a practical, down to earth flavour and, as their titles suggest, they do not make light of the difficulties and disruption that following Christ brings.

Poet and visionary that he was, Matheson had no time for those Christians who remained always up the "glorious mountains" of mysticism and never descended into the plain to share their vision with ordinary believers. As he puts it in "The Practicalness of Christ's Cross", to bear the body of the dying Christ in your life is "to come from high thought into menial action. It is to empty thyself into the commonplace. It is to descend into what men call reality."

1. Interrupted Communion

"Go, get thee down; for thy people, which thou broughtest out of the land of Egypt, have corrupted themselves." Exodus 32:7

"Go, get thee down;" it was surely a hard, an unlikely mandate. Was it not a command to go forth from the secret of God's pavilion, from the Mount of Divine vision and Divine communion into the vision of things that were not Divine, into communion with things that were not holy? You and I have been forced at times to feel what Moses felt. We have had moments of rapture, in which we have been allowed to stand on the very top of the mountain and to see, as it were, the face of God unveiled – moments when His countenance was radiant as the light and His raiment dazzling as the sunlit snow. But presently a cloud has fallen over the vision and the glory has vanished from the scene. The rapture is turned into coldness, and the mountain sinks into a common plain, filled with the concourse of the multitude, and echoing with the cries of human struggle; a voice has sounded in mine ear and said, "Go, get thee down."

Yes, my soul, and has it not brought to thine ear the reason of its sounding? Why has it commanded thee to quit the glorious mountain for the common plain? It is because it *is* a common plain. It is because on that plain there is a concourse of living beings who are unfit for the glorious mountain. They have no vision from a height, and therefore they are oppressed by life's labour and its ladenness. They want some one to heal them, some one to lift them, some one to inspire them with the breath of a presence that has dwelt aloft. Thou mayest be that presence. If thou hast gazed on the face of God, thou hast a mesmeric passport into the heart of thy brother man. He shall lift up his eyes unto the hills, whence cometh *thine* aid; make no tarrying to go down, O my soul.

Moments on the Mount

2. The Trouble Brought by Christ

"When Herod the king had heard these things, he was troubled." Matthew 2:3

There were four kingdoms congregated at the Christian dawn – the kingdom of nature, the kingdom of knowledge, the kingdom of worldliness, and the kingdom of unworldliness. The kingdom of nature came in a star, the kingdom of knowledge in the Magi, the kingdom of wordliness in Herod, and the kingdom of unworldliness in the child-Christ. Only one of the kingdoms was troubled by the child. Nature did not fear Him, knowledge did not shun Him; Herod alone trembled at His coming.

My soul, art thou afraid of the coming of Christ into thy life? Dost thou fear that He will narrow thee? Nay, but He will narrow that which narrows thee. He will not destroy thy love of nature, for He is the crown of nature. He will not dispute thy right to knowledge, for He is the end of knowledge; but He will expel from thy heart the Herod that imprisons thee. He will deny the power of Herod to make thee happy, and He will prove His denial even by thy pain. Wouldst thou rather be without that pain? Hast thou forgotten the pool of Bethesda? An angel came down to trouble the waters, and then the waters were powerful. Thou, too, shalt be powerful after thou hast been troubled. Thinkest thou that the stillness of primeval chaos was a calm? There was no calm till the Spirit moved. Only when the face of the waters

is ruffled by the breath of the life Divine is the
mandate truly heard, "Let there be light."

Moments on the Mount

3. The Place in Christ for Repentance

"Jesus saw a man, named Matthew, sitting at the receipt of custom: and He saith unto him, Follow Me." Matthew 9:9

There is one peculiarity with which I have been struck in the calls of Jesus; they are not preceded by any denunciation of the man's past life. The Baptist's *were;* his initial cry is, "Repent!" Jesus, indeed, calls to a life which *involves* repentance; but repentance is not His initial cry. Not even is it so in the parable of the prodigal son; the Father gives His demonstration of love before any expression of sin on the part of the prodigal. He sees him afar off, He has compassion, He runs across the intervening space to meet him, He folds him in His arms and lavishes on him His affection ere ever one word of contrition falls from his lips.

In the case of Matthew we should have expected the first note of Jesus to have been reproach. Matthew had been living voluntarily the life of a slave. He had become the truculent servant of Roman masters and had wrung for them the tribute from his countrymen. Should we not expect the first cry of Jesus to have been, "Think shame of yourself!" It is not; it is, "Follow Me!"

Can we account for this? Yes, it shows His profound wisdom and how much deeper He sees than the world sees. The world thinks that a man begins by repenting and then turns to follow the right way. It is the reverse. He begins by following the right way and then he repents of being so long on the wrong one. It is not our sorrow for the past that leads us to form a beautiful ideal; it is our reception of a beautiful ideal that leads us to sorrow for the past. Matthew does not say, "I have led an ignoble life and must now see Christ"; he says, "I have seen Christ, and therefore I know that my life has been ignoble."

God's first season for every converted man is the summer. He is not at once shown the winter of his own soul; he is plunged at first into the Divine radiance. He only learns his rags by seeing the new garment that is to clothe him. He never knows his pool to be stagnant till he stands by the great sea. It is when the waves wash his feet, when the spray refreshes his countenance, when the swell of ocean murmurs in his ear, that he remembers the inland pool of yesterday and cries, "These were not living waters!"

Lord, let mine be the call of Matthew – the call into summer radiance! Let me not say within my heart, "I dare not come; I have not a sufficient sense of my own inadequacy"! Teach me that the sense of my own inadequacy can only be born in Thy light, only perfected in heaven! I have always thought the knowledge of my sin a *beginner's* lesson; reveal to me that it is the lesson for the highest class of Christian! I shall only become dissatisfied when I reach Thy grace; therefore let Thy grace be my earliest seeking! Let me not begin by trying to feel my corruption! Let not my first journey be an inspection of my own quagmire! Let it be a flight over the ocean of Thy love! Let me soar at once to the crystal fountain, to the river of life, to the streets of gold! Let not my opening thought be of my tabernacles of clay; let it fly up to the gates of pearl and the rainbow of emerald and the skies without night! Make not my first voyage retrospective; let me begin, not with the past, but with the future! Let the earliest voice I hear be the voice Matthew heard – ''Follow Me''! Be *Thou* my beginning, O Lord! Let me enter Thy temple by the gate called Beautiful! Bring me at once into Thy summer, today into Thy paradise!

Rests by the River

4. The Practicalness of Christ's Cross

"Always bearing about in the body the dying of the Lord Jesus, that the life also of Jesus might be made manifest in our body." 2 Corinthians 4:10

What an unhealthy state of mind! you say – to be ever fondling the idea of death. How can it manifest life to bear death in my body? Will it not sap my energy? Will it not make me a dreamer? Will I not lose all interest in the present world, if I am always thinking of passing from earth to heaven? Yes; but this is no common death of which the apostle speaks; it is the dying of the Lord Jesus. The dying of the Lord Jesus was not the passing from earth to heaven; it was the passing from heaven to earth. Every step of His dying was a step downwards. He took the servant's form. He took the human likeness. He took the fleeting fashion of a man. He took the image of the *humblest* man. He went down deeper than humility. He lost His personality in love. He became one with the poor, the outcast, the erring. He felt the pains that dwelt in other bodies, the griefs that lived in other souls, the sins that slept in other hearts. At last He touched the lowest ground, and, therefore, the common ground – He completed His dying in the Cross. It was the final stage of His union with man. It brought Him into the heart of the world. It made Him in the deepest sense a citizen of time.

Say not, then, oh, my soul, that to bear Christ's dying within thee is to lose thy hold of earth; it is to double that hold. It is to come from high thought into menial action. It is to empty thyself into the commonplace. It is to descend into what men call reality. It is to leave the green fields of speculation for the thorny paths of practice. It is to give up thy poetry for other people's prose, to resign thy sunlight for thy weak brother's candle. Art thou prepared for this sacrifice, oh, my soul? It wants not less but more love of the world. When Jesus died he went to Galilee. Only in death did He touch the uttermost earth. If thou wouldst bear in thy body His dying, thou must love not death but life. Nothing but the preciousness of life could prompt the dying of the Lord Jesus, or prompt thee to follow that dying. Thou canst not reach it by dreaming; thou must put away thy dream. Thine eye must be fixed on the rude multitude. Thine ear must be caught by the cry of sorrow. Thy hand must be held by the clasp of pain. Thou must dismiss the thought of delectable mountains, or of harps on the glassy sea. Thou must consider the sea that is not glassy, the mountains that are not delectable, the sounds that are not music. Thine must be the love of the prosaic present. If thou wouldst long to depart and be with Christ, it must be, like Him, to get nearer to the earth, closer to the wants of man. To leave the world that is beyond for the world of the passing day – that is the dying of the Lord Jesus.

Searchings in the Silence

5. Instinctive Christians

"That ye may be found of Him in peace." 2 Peter 3:14

There are two sets of minds in the Christian life – those who find Christ, and those whom Christ finds. Those who find Christ are active; those who are found by Christ are passive. The one have a hard struggle; the other enter the gates "in peace". There are some whose experience is that of the wise men of the east; they search for the star, and discover it after many days. There are others like the keepers of the flock of Bethlehem; they are engaged in their own work, and the star comes to *them*. The men of the east are men of talent; they plan, and they succeed. But the keepers of the flock are men of genius; they never need to plan; they are illuminated in a moment. In the midst of their daily toil there is suddenly with them a multitude of the heavenly host singing "glory". They are like the great masters in music; their work costs them little trouble. They are born to love; they are made to sacrifice; they are bound to say the right thing at the right time. The garment of goodness becomes them, sits gracefully on them. It is a garment, not of heaviness, but of praise. The men who are found by Christ take the kingdom by violence.

Son of Man, I would like to be one of Thy men of genius – one of those who are *found* by Thee. I would like Thy life to be my starting-point

115

rather than my goal. I would rather fly *with* Thee than *to* Thee. I do not want to wait for Thy rest till the end of the journey; I want to journey on Thy wing. I would have rest before I start – rest to help my start, rest to sustain my start. It is by Thy rest I would travel; I would walk by rest, run by rest, fly by rest. If I come first to seek Thee, I shall be weary when I find Thee; however short the way, it is too long without Thee. Shall I ask the wings of a dove, that I may fly away and be at rest? Nay; let me get Thy rest, and then I shall have the wings. There is no power of motion like the repose in Thee. The brooding of Thy Spirit is a rushing, mighty wind; it will carry me beyond myself – into the life of my brother. Come, then, to me, oh, Dove of the Firmament. Wait not till I seek Thee, amid the troubles of the wilderness. Descend upon me at the dawn. Light upon me when the heavens are opened, and the waters of youth are sparkling. Abide on me when it is morning and the day is yet to begin. Spread Thy wings over me before I go out into the temptation. Bring Thy message of peace, and I shall be strengthened for every war. I shall find myself when I am found by Thee.

Searchings in the Silence

VI
Christian
Freedom

VI Christian Freedom

Christians follow him in whose service they find perfect freedom. Through total obedience they come to have the blessed liberty of the children of God. This apparent paradox stands at the heart of the Christian faith which seems to demand total commitment and yet promise utter freedom. In the brief section that follows this paradox is explored in meditation, prayer and verse.

1. Unselfish Moments

"And the Lord turned the captivity of Job when he prayed for his friends." Job 42:10

It is only in moments of unselfishness that I am free. The iron chain that binds me is the thought of myself and of my own calamities; if I could but be liberated from that, my captivity would be turned in an hour. If, under the shadow of the cloud, I could but remember that the shadow of the same cloud hovers over my brother-man, the vision of his shadow would destroy mine. In the moment of prayer for him my burden would fall from me. I would seek it, and lo! it would not be found; it would be as if it had not been.

O Thou Divine Spirit of self-forgetfulness, Spirit of Christ, Spirit of the Cross, it is in Thee alone that I can find this freedom. Liberate me from myself, and instead of the iron chain, give me a chain of gold. It is not the chain that lowers me, it is the material of which it is made; it is not the sorrow that makes me a captive, it is the centring of the sorrow round my own life. Help me to take up the burdens of others. Help me to know what it is to have rest in bearing an additional yoke, Thy yoke, the yoke of humanity. Help me to feel what it is to have peace in carrying a new care, Thy care, the care of universal love. Help me to learn what it is to be transfigured in the prayer for others; to have the countenance shining as the light, and the raiment white and glistering.

Moments on the Mount

2. The Fetters of the Spirit

"And now, behold, I am going to Jerusalem, bound in the Spirit, not knowing what shall befall me there" Acts 20:22

Spirit of Christ, Thy chain is golden. The fetters Thou imposest are wings of freedom. There is no liberty like the liberty of being bound to go. When Thou layest upon me the sense of obligation, that moment Thou settest my spirit free. When Thou sayest that I must, my heart says, "I can." My strength is proportionate to the strength of those cords that bind me. I am never so unrestrained as when I am constrained by Thy love. Evermore, Thou divine Spirit, guide me by this instinct of the right. Put round about my heart the cord of Thy captivating love and draw me whither in my own light I would not go. Bind me to Thyself as Thou bindest the planets to the sun, that it may become the very law of my nature to be led by Thee. May I be content to know that goodness and mercy shall *follow* me without waiting to see them in advance of me. May I be content to feel that my God shall be my rearward without folding my hands till I find Him in the van. My journey to Jerusalem shall be fraught with power when in the strength of the Spirit I am bound to go.

Voices of the Spirit

3. Christian Freedom

"Paul, the prisoner of Jesus Christ." Ephesians 3:2

Make me a captive, Lord,
  And then I shall be free;
Force me to render up my sword,
  And I shall conqueror be.
I sink in life's alarms
  When by myself I stand;
Imprison me within Thine arms,
  And strong shall be my hand.

2 My heart is weak and poor
    Until it master find;
  It has no spring of action sure –
    It varies with the wind.
  It cannot freely move
    Till Thou hast wrought its chain;
  Enslave it with Thy matchless love,
    And deathless it shall reign.

3 My power is faint and low
    Till I have learned to serve;
  It wants the needed fire to glow,
    It wants the breeze to nerve;
  It cannot drive the world
    Until itself be driven;
  Its flag can only be unfurled
    When Thou shalt breathe from heaven.

4 My will is not my own
      Till Thou has made it Thine;
   If it would reach a monarch's throne
      It must its crown resign;
   It only stands unbent
      Amid the clashing strife
   When on Thy bosom it has leant
      And found in Thee its life.

Sacred Songs

VII
Solitude

VII Solitude

To be blind is inevitably to be cut off in some degree from the world and from others. George Matheson experienced periods of intense loneliness which must have been intensified by the fact that he never married. His meditation "Ties for the Solitary" has a special poignancy in its call on God to "make straight not in the desert, but on the highway, a path for those who walk alone". It also seems almost to suggest that solitude is almost a vocation, a state like celibacy which makes it easier to surrender to God and to feel deeply for the whole of suffering humanity.

A rather different value in being alone is explored in the poem, "The Revealing Solitude". Here Matheson the mystic and spiritual pilgrim is to the fore, seeking to climb the lonely heights which were scaled by the spiritual giants of the past.

1. Ties for the Solitary

"God setteth the solitary in families." Psalm 68:6

There are some lives to whom the nuptial torch is denied. They form no family ties, and, as the ties into which they were born are dissolved, one fears that they will be alone. They need not be. "God setteth the solitary in families." Religion supplies the place of marriage. Often have I thought of these words of the Master, "Whosoever shall do the will of My Father, which is in heaven, the same is My brother, and sister, and mother." The soul surrendered to God is brother, sister, mother, to the race of Man.

Who, think you, of merely human birth, had the widest heart for earthly ties? Was it not the solitary man of Tarsus? Who speaks of the family like *him?* Who legislates for the household like him? Who feels for the bereaved like him? And why? Because they who are united to Christ are wedded also to humanity. They have the ring and the robe. They have the bridal garment. They have the marriage supper of the Lamb. They have the cares of all households, the weight of all children, the guidance of all youth, the help of all manhood, the support of all age. It is a crowded life to be married like the *angels*.

Oh Thou who hast consecrated not only the nuptial torch but the want of it, make room for the solitary lives. Make straight not in the desert, but on the highway, a path for those who walk alone. Invite the virgin souls of earth to the marriage supper of the Lamb. Kindle the paternal instinct in the heart that is no father. Light the family altar in the home that has no ties. Fill with the voices of the multitude the spaces left vacant by the brethren. Replenish the isles with Thy fulness – the fulness of human sympathy. Give a crowded interest to spirits outside the crowd. Bring the vision of the city into the silence of the garden. Put the burden of all souls on the life that has no burden. Lay the debt of humanity on those who know not lesser bonds. The isles wait for Thee to make them vocal. When Thou hast set the solitary in families there shall be no more seas.

Searchings in the Silence

2. The Revealing Solitude

"When they were alone, He expounded all things to his disciples" Mark 4:34

There is a solitude whose waste
    Is empty not to me,
For there upon the heart are traced
    The sights no eye can see,
And in the seeming void I stand
In contact with Immanuel's land.

2 I would not change that solitude
    For gleaming pearls of gold,
For 'tis the holy ground where stood
    The Master's feet of old;
'Twas from the reach of upper air
He bore the weight of human care.

3 'Tis not the dwellers on the plain
    That feel their comrades' load;
'Tis only from the mountain-chain
    We mark the winding road;
The mystic heights alone receive
The common clouds of those that grieve.

4 I would not be alone with God
    To be the less with man;
I would not rest in His abode
    To shun the race I ran:
I only crave an hour above
That I may deeper sink, through love.

5 I long to scale the lonely height
    Where Moses' footprints lie,

For all my meekness in the fight
   Is borrowed from on high;
And only in that higher birth
I bear the storm and stress of earth.

6 I long to scale the lonely height
   Where Abram's faith was sealed,
For only in the depth of night
   Is perfect love revealed;
And in the steps of sacrifice
I find the earth-path to the skies.

7 I long to scale the lonely height
   Where Jesus climbed His cross,
For only is life's glory bright
   When gain is found in loss;
And earth unites with heaven above
When death becomes undying love.

Sacred Songs

VIII
The Passing
Years

VIII   The Passing Years

Although the meditations and poems in this section do not belong to the last years of Matheson's life, they show a clear consciousness of the advancing years. They range from the impassioned plea to "give me back my youth" in the opening prayer to rather more considered reflections on the greater vision and even the optimism that comes with old age contained in the three meditations. It is perhaps worth explaining that the Biblical story which inspires "Vision in Old Age" is the account of Moses being led up Mount Nebo at the age of 120 to survey the promised land just before his death.

The two poems in this section beautifully express the Christian view that love never wearies or grows old and that death, far from bringing life to an end and snuffing out consciousness, in fact brings a clearer vision and heralds a new youth.

1. The Glory of Morning

"And in the morning you shall see the glory of the Lord" Exodus 16:7

My God, give me back my youth; I can regain it in Thee. Let the shadows of my life be rekindled into morning's glow, let my heart be lit with Thine eternal youth. Thou hast promised us eternal life, and what is that? Not merely life for ever, but life for ever young. Thine eternal life can make me a child again, a child without childishness. O Thou, on whose bloom time breathes not, who art the same yesterday, and today, and for ever, bathe me in those fountains of the morning whence Thou hast the dew of Thy youth. Bathe me in the ocean of that love in which there is no variableness nor the least shadow of turning, that the pulses of this heart may be renewed. Then shall I have the bright and morning star, and the dayspring from on high shall rise within me. Then shall creation break forth into gladness, as in the day when the morning stars sang together, and all the sons of God shouted for joy; I shall see the glory of life when Thy morning is in my soul.

Moments on the Mount

2. Vision in Old Age

"His eye was not dim, nor his natural force abated." Deuteronomy 34:7

Most of us have our brightest visions in the days of our youth. The time when men commonly stand on Mount Nebo is the hour of life's morning; it is then that the promised land appears most glorious, it is then that the prospective eye is least dimmed by experience. But this man Moses was an exception to the rule; his vision came in old age. The days of his youth and manhood had been too prosaic for poetic flights. They had been days of danger, days of anxiety, days of burden-bearing, days of commonplace annoyances, more hard to endure because they *were* commonplace. It was only at the last that his child-life came. It was only amid the twilight shadows that there rose to him that vision which men are wont to behold at morning – the vision of coming glory, the prospect of a promised land. His age of anticipation began where his age of experience ended, his inner man was renewed where his outer man was about to perish. In the vigour of manhood, in front of the burning fire of God, he had felt his vision dim; in the extremity of old age he had neither a doubt nor a fear. "His eye was not dim, nor his natural force abated."

My soul, if thou couldst live this life of sacrifice, thou too wouldst have a vision in the hour of death. There is a life whose natural force is not abated with the years; it grows stronger when other things fade. ''Whether there be prophecies, they shall fail; whether there be tongues, they shall cease; whether there be knowledge, it shall vanish away; but love never faileth.'' It is the Nebo of old age, the height from which amid surrounding ruins the heart surveys its promised land. That height of certainty may be thine. If love be in thee, it will survive all things. Memory may fade, fancy may droop, judgment may waver, perception may languish, but the eye of the heart shall grow brighter toward the close. That which men have called ''the valley'' shall be to thee a mountain. Thou shalt face the setting sun, and shalt see in it a new rising. The clouds that environ the intellect shall break before the childhood of the spirit, and amid the snows of winter thy time for the singing of birds shall come. Thou shalt gaze upon a world's dissolving views, and say, ''O death, where is thy sting? O grave, where is thy victory?''

Moments on the Mount

3. The Ripest Communion

"Unto Thee, O Lord, do I lift up my soul." Psalm 35:1

There are three upliftings in the religious life –
hope, faith, and love. Hope is the lifting up of
the eyes; it is the time of youth. There is always
a charm in unfinishedness when we are young;
the unreached land is the desired land. Faith is
the lifting up of the hands; it is the time of
manhood. Every lifting of the man's hand is a
seed sown in faith. He is in all things a
speculator; he trusts to the mercy of the coming
day. Love is the lifting up of the soul; it is the
time of age.

I have always felt that the autumn of life is
the season in which we first view things as they
are. Hope and faith are in the future; love is in
the present. The eye looks forward; the hand
stretches onward; but the soul never moves from
its place; it admires here and now. To have the
soul lifted up to God is what men commonly call
death. The Psalmist says we can reach it without
dying, can reach it today, this moment, by one
flight of love. Love is the true lifting of the soul
– the true death. It brings me from time into
eternity, from the changeful into the abiding.
It raises me into a world where there is no
future, no tomorrow, no wish to look forward
– where the Divine *presence* is fulness of joy.
It makes me independent of memory,
independent of hope, independent of change.
It restores to me the life of the butterfly; it
magnifies the moment; it bids the sun stand still.

It is the end of all climbing, the close of all longing, the satisfaction of all aspiring, the goal of all seeking – the rest that remaineth to the people of God.

Son of Man, lift up my soul. There is no need to wait for death; death lifts not so high as love. Love is the swiftest of all flights into Thy presence. I know why John lay on Thy bosom; because he had the most rapid wing. Hope is beautiful, but it cannot rest; it will not let Peter make a tabernacle for Thee. Faith is beautiful, but it cannot rest; it bids Paul press forward for the mark of Thy prize. But love reposes. It rests on Thy bosom because it is *Thy* bosom – because it can dream of nothing beyond. The uplifted eye has an expanse before it; the uplifted hand has a work before it; but the uplifted soul basks in Thy present glory. It says Thy will be done. It buries prayer in praise. It loses Thy rainbow in Thy Ararat. It forgets the thought of tomorrow in the rest of today. I shall say "*Now* is the accepted time" when Thou hast lifted up my soul.

Searchings in the Silence

4. The Fadeless Thing

"What shall I do that I may inherit eternal life?"
Mark 10:17

Tell me a thing that never grows old
  All through the day, all through the day,
Keeps without dimness its youth and its gold
  All through the length of the day;
Beauty grows pale with the flight of the years,
Gladness must fail when the heart has its fears;
Is there a life where no shadow appears
  All through the length of the day?

2 There is a life that remains ever young
  All through the day, all through the day,
Singing at evening the song it has sung
  All through the length of the day;
Love is the glory that never grows old,
Telling the story a hundred times told,
Keeping its light where the shadows have
    rolled,
  All through the length of the day.

3 Love has no record of time on its brow
  All through the day, all through the day,
Keeps the first freshness of life's morning vow
  All through the length of the day;
Strong in its power 'mid the snow-flakes of age,
Full in its flower while the winter blasts rage,
Bearing a fire that no damp can assuage,
  All through the length of the day.

4 Give me, O Father, this best gift of Thine,
    All through the day, all through the day,
That in eternity's light I may shine
    All through the length of the day;
Wearing my youth like an evergreen flower,
Guarding the truth of my bright childhood's
    hour,
Shrining my soul in an unfading bower,
    All through the length of the day.

5 And when the forests of earth shall be bare
    All through the day, all through the day,
Gleamings of glory and peace shall be there
    All through the length of the day;
Down in the valley the mount shall appear,
Sunlight shall rally the ranks of the year,
Life at the portals of death shall be near,
    All through the length of the day.

Sacred Songs

5. The Hopefulness of St. Paul

"Experience worketh hope" Romans 5:4

Does it? I would have expected Paul to say just the contrary. If this is a world of sin and misery, ought it not to seem blacker as we pass through it? And yet the facts appear to make for Paul. Who are they that take the gloomiest view of life? Is it the aged, the infirm, the wayworn? No; it is the young – the men who are setting out upon their journey. Youth is called the age of hope – and so it is; but it is not hope for this world. It is the dream of a fairy scene far away. For things as they are, youth has no mercy; they are too prosaic, too common, too unclean. Paul himself was a pessimist in youth; his hopes were for other worlds than ours. To be with Christ was to be "caught up in the air" – borne beyond the scene. But, as the road advanced, the shadows faded. The song of the earth-birds became beautiful with the winding of the way. The fields of time grew greener with the westering of life's sun. The light of Damascus left the air and began to illuminate the housetops, and the experience that threatened to work despair became the parent of hope.

And so, my Father, Thy world is not so bad a place after all. It looks gloomier at the entering than at the ending gate. Thou hast a special harp for those that have walked upon the sea. In the days of my youth I sang to the scenes of fancy, but my latest harp shall be for reality. I shall sing

143

to the praise of the six days' creation when I have reached the Sabbath. Put Thy new song in my mouth, oh! my Father – the song of Moses and the Lamb, the song of the desert and the Cross. Reveal to me the gold beneath the dust, the fire within the flint, the flowers around the clay. Reveal to me the beauty of common things, nay, of painful things. Reveal to me the romance of real life, the heroism of daily toil, the power of prosaic sacrifice. Show me the prospect from the west gate of the temple – the gate near to the setting sun. I have looked long enough from the east – the delusive light of morning. I have been seeking a heaven beyond experience, and the chords of my harp have been broken; they shall be strung to a nobler strain when experience itself worketh hope.

Searchings in the Silence

6. Life in Death

"His eye was not dim, nor his natural force abated." Deuteronomy 34:7

There is a life whose vital power
   Grows stronger as the hill descends;
It sleeps in nature's morning hour;
   It wakes where nature ends.

2 I saw a mighty soul of earth
   Go down into the vale to die,
And one by one the gifts of birth
   Reclaimed were by the sky.

3 I saw the daylight leave the walls;
   I heard the music fade away,
And through the aisles of memory's halls
   The echoes ceased to stray.

4 But in the temple's inner shrine
   There burned a glory sevenfold bright,
And, like a lighthouse lashed with brine,
   Faith streamed into the night.

5 Men said, "He is unconscious now";
   God said, "For the first time he knows";
The vision of the mountain's brow
   Is clearest at life's close.

6 O golden morn at closing day,
   O youth revived at gates of even,
O spring-time born of year's decay,
   We hail thy pledge of heaven!

7 We hail the pledge that something lives
    When heart and flesh are faint and frail,
  When earthly joy no pleasure gives
    And human pomp is pale –

8 That even then with undimmed gaze
    My soul amid the waste can stand,
  And by the light of larger rays
    Discern the promised land!

Sacred Songs

IX
One in Christ

IX   One in Christ

George Matheson's broad and liberal ecumenical sympathies extended not just to every branch of the Christian Church but embraced other faiths as well. He firmly believed that if Jesus Christ was, indeed, "all in all", then Christianity should embrace and enfold all the great religions of the world. In the pages that follow his sense that all are one in Christ is explored in a poem that uses the image of islands being turned into one great land mass, in an extract from a work of academic theology and in a magnificent set of verses which I strongly recommend singing to the tune of 'Abide with me'!

1. Island Moments

"The isles shall wait for me." Isaiah 60:9

The isles, the isles shall wait;
　　They most of all shall weary,
For they cannot find a gate
　　Through the ocean vast and dreary;
They hear the waters moan
　　From dawn to dark around them,
And they feel themselves alone
　　In the bands where fate has bound them.

2　The island lives shall wait,
　　The lives by sorrow branded;
The rocks beneath were great,
　　And their ship of hope was stranded;
And others passed them by,
　　In the race of life excelling,
Till besides the sea and sky
　　There was none looked near their dwelling.

3　We all have island hours,
　　We all have moments lonely,
Wherein 'mid faded flowers
　　We dwell in Patmos only;
The silence brooding there,
　　With the calm sea dividing,
Is harder far to bear
　　Than storms in fury riding.

4　And then, how sweet to know
　　That o'er this cruel ocean
An unseen bridge doth go
　　Supporting love's devotion,

That one great heart doth span
   The intervening spaces,
And link the isles of man
   To all the joyful races.

5 O Christ of mighty love,
   O Heart of human feeling,
Still through the waters move
   To grant Thy bright revealing!
In hollow of Thy hand
   These waters Thou constrainest,
And we have reached dry land
   Where Thou with us remainest.

6 If Thou abide with me,
   I too have joined my brother,
For all are one in Thee
   And each is bound to other.
Thou takest up the isles,
   Thou bindest souls that sever,
And all dividing miles
   Are bridged in Thee for ever.

Sacred Songs

2. Christianity and the Messages of the Past

Is it possible that the religions of the past may themselves be included in the Christian message of reconciliation? Is it conceivable that Christianity has furnished a ground for peace not only within but without its own fold? Paul says that in Christ "all things stand together"; and it is a most remarkable statement. It seems to suggest that the angles of opposing faiths are rubbed off when they stand in the Christian temple, and that ideas once mutually conflicting can there rest side by side. Do not misunderstand me. I do not for a moment imagine that the first Christians said to themselves, "We shall found a religion which shall embrace the faiths of the world." I do not suppose that any one of these disciples had ever heard of Brahmanism, or Buddhism, or Parseeism. But this does not even touch the question. These religions are representative of certain ideas which belong to human nature. If a religion appears which professes to be a universal faith, it must show its universality by uniting these ideas. It must be a ladder reaching from earth unto heaven, each of whose ascending steps shall find a place for one of the systems of the past. Instead of being manifested to reveal the falsity of former views, it must, for the first time, vindicate the truth of all, – must discover a point in which beliefs hitherto deemed at variance may lie down together in unity, and receive from the heart of man a common justification.

It is popularly said that Christianity has conquered the faiths of the past. And so it has;

but in a very peculiar way. It has conquered as the Roman empire wished to conquer – not by submergence, but by incorporation. It would not be true to say that it has destroyed them; it would be more correct to affirm that it has kept them alive. They had all outgrown their youth, all survived their time, all failed to bring rest to the soul. The form remained; the sensuous life remained; but the spirit had passed away. If Christianity had not appeared, paradoxical as it may seem, I think these religious would have become supremely uninteresting; Christianity has made them vivid by making them living. In its many-sidedness it has a side for each of these. It has let in its light upon them; it has given its breath to them; it has found a place for them in its own system. It has given them a logical order which has dispelled the contradictions of the natural order. Indian and Greek, Roman and Teuton, Buddhist and Parsee, Egyptian and Chinaman, can meet here hand in hand; because in the comprehensive temple of Christian truth there is not only a niche which each may fill, but a niche which, at some stage of its development, must be filled by one and all.

Therefore it is that the religion of Christ ought to have peculiar interest in the faiths of the past. They are not, to her, dead faiths; they are not even modernized. They are preserved inviolable as parts of herself – more inviolable than they would have been if she had never come. China may keep her materialism, and India may retain her mysticism; Rome may grasp her strength, and Greece may nurse her beauty; Persia may tell of the opposition to God's power, and Egypt

153

may sing of His pre-eminence even amid the tombs: but for each and all there is a seat in the Christian Pantheon, and a justification in the light of the manifold wisdom of God.

The Distinctive Messages of the Old Religions

3. One in Christ

"That in the dispensation of the fulness of times He might gather together in one all things in Christ." Ephesians 1:10

Gather us in, Thou Love that fillest all!
  Gather our rival faiths within Thy fold!
Rend each man's temple veil and bid it fall,
  That we may know that Thou hast been of old;
    Gather us in!

2 Gather us in! we worship only Thee;
  In varied names we stretch a common hand;
In diverse forms a common soul we see;
  In many ships we seek one spirit-land;
    Gather us in!

3 Each sees one colour of Thy rainbow-light,
  Each looks upon one tint and calls it heaven;
Thou art the fulness of our partial sight;
  We are not perfect till we find the seven;
    Gather us in!

4 Thine is the mystic life great India craves,
  Thine is the Parsee's sin-destroying beam,
Thine is the Buddhist's rest from tossing
    waves,
  Thine is the empire of vast China's dream;
    Gather us in!

5 Thine is the Roman's strength without his
    pride,
  Thine is the Greek's glad world without its
    graves,

Thine is Judea's law with love beside,
The truth that censures and the grace that
saves;
Gather us in!

6 Some seek a Father in the heavens above,
Some ask a human image to adore,
Some crave a spirit vast as life and love:
Within Thy mansions we have all and more;
Gather us in!

Sacred Songs

X
Finding Our Rest in God

X Finding Our Rest in God

For all his stress on sacrifice, the strongly practical bent to his Christianity and his sense that God was to be found in the clouds as much as in the sunshine, George Matheson was ultimately possessed by a secure and confident faith that the destiny of the human soul was to find its rest with God. He was haunted by that powerful image in Psalm 84 of the sparrow finding a home and the swallow a nest while humans longed to find their dwelling place with the Lord. Again and again in the writings that appear on the following pages he portrays man alone among God's creatures in being somehow restless and unfulfilled on this earth. This is particularly the theme of his meditation "Human Unrest" and his poem "The Unfulfilled Desire".

The later meditations concentrate more directly on the heavenly home that Our Lord is preparing for us. They contain some striking phrases, like the suggestion that the furniture in the celestial city will be homely rather than gorgeous, an idea that echoes Dame Julian of Norwich's stress on the homeliness of Jesus in her *Revelations of Divine Love*.

This section and indeed this book ends with George Matheson's masterpiece of devotional writing, "O Love that wilt not let me go", in which he draws together so many of his favourite themes and images – self-sacrifice, the promise of the cloud and rain, the depth and infinity of the ocean and the resting place that the weary human soul finds in God.

1. Human Unrest

"As the hart panteth after the water brooks, so panteth my soul after Thee, O God." Psalm 42:1

All things live in their own element – the cattle on the plain, the fish in the sea, the bird in the air. Thy element is God. Thou art the only creature in this universe that art not now *in* thine element; thou art an anomaly in the order of creation. The sparrow hath an house and the swallow a nest for herself, but thou longest, faintest; thou hast not found a resting-place in all the tabernacles of time. Thou art the least happy of all creatures. The bird carols in the air all the day, but thou hast not a day quite undimmed by tears.

Why is it thus with thee? Wherefore art thou less happy than the beast of the field? Is it because thou hast fewer resources? Nay, it is because thy resources are greater, because they are too great for the world that environs thee. It is because thou art not living in thine element, and the element in which thou livest is not adequate to thy powers. Thou hast capacities for boundless flight, and thou art chained within a limited area; thou art made for God, and thou art narrowed to the dust.

No wonder thou art not happy; it is thy greatness makes thee unhappy. If thou hadst been a bird of the air thou wouldst have carolled like him, but because thou art more thou hast no unclouded song. And yet thou wert made for song. Thou wert not only made for song in a future world, thou wert designed for it here.

Thou art promising thyself joy in regions beyond the grave, but the only element that can give thee joy is on both sides of the grave. Thy joy is God, and God is here as well as there. The atmosphere of the Divine surrounds thee *now*. Thou needst not wait for death to reach it; thou canst soar into it at any moment.

Say not that others have their portion here, but that thou hast thy portion hereafter; is not thy portion eternity, and is not eternity now as well as then? Thy portion is here, my soul, – on the threshold of thy life, at the door of thy being; it is *in* the earth, though it is not of the earth. Why shouldst thou pant any more? The river that makes glad the city of God can make glad the cities of men. Thou canst find thine element as easily as the hart findeth the water brooks. "Ho, every one that thirsteth, come ye to the waters."

Moments on the Mount

2. The Unfulfilled Desire

"Delight thyself also in the Lord; and He shall gives thee the desires of thine heart." Psalm 37:4

Father, my heart has never found
　　Its perfect goal below;
It beats in vain upon the ground
　　Against the cold and snow;
It has no chance to reach its home
Save in a kingdom yet to come.

2　All other things beneath the sky
　　　Receive their kingdom here;
There is a splendour for the eye,
　　　A music for the ear;
But my heart's cry for perfect love
Waits to be heard in heaven above.

3　Why should my heart alone be void
　　　If earth to man be all!
Why should Thy bounty be alloyed
　　　By one unanswered call!
Wings help the bird's desire for flight;
Why should my soul be left in night!

4　Thy wings are coming, O my heart!
　　　Thy want of them on earth
Itself is promise that thou art
　　　Prepared for higher birth.
The need this world has so denied
Is bound above to be supplied.

5 Thou hast not found thy sphere in life –
   Only thy hemisphere;
One half thy globe is mist and strife;
   The other must be clear.
Thou shalt be rounded in the day
When God shall wipe thy tears away.

6 Within thy breast thou canst not plant
   A flower of fadeless breath,
For some are chilled by frost and want,
   And all must yield to death;
Thou waitest for a higher hour
To lend thee room to wield thy power.

7 Sure as the eye demands its beam,
   Sure as the ear its voice,
So surely on thy path shall gleam
   The freedom of thy choice;
And thou to whom earth was not given
Shalt meet thy counterpart in heaven.

Sacred Songs

3. The Ground for Spiritual Anxiety

"Shall not the day of the Lord be darkness, and not light?" Amos 5:20

The prophet is speaking to men who have a good religious creed but are living a bad life. They are committing every vice under the sun and praying for the day of the Lord. Amos says they are praying against themselves – asking something which, to them, would be darkness and not light. He does not mean that when the day of the Lord comes the wicked will be prevented from seeing it. His words imply the contrary. He says distinctly that if the day of the Lord came tomorrow it would embrace under its dome the bad as well as the good. But he says that to the bad and to the good it would have a different appearance. Both would look on the same thing, but they would have a contrary perception; what was light to the good would be darkness to the bad.

To a selfish man there would be no place in the universe so miserable as heaven. What makes heaven day to Jesus would make it night to Judas – the reign of love. I have been often struck with the question Hosea puts to selfish people, "What shall ye do in the day of the feast of the Lord?" He does not say they will get no place at the table; he asks what interest they will have in the proceedings when they sit down. How will they appreciate a banquet where every sentiment proposed will be commemorative of sacrifice, and every plaudit raised will be a tribute to the Lamb that was slain! It is not

165

enough to be free from so-called adverse circumstances. The deepest adversity is solitude of soul – the want of harmony with one's environment. It is not enough that I am untouched by the lightning; I must be touched by the sunbeam. I would rather be struck by lightning than struck by nothing, for the soul is dead that slumbers, and the chords that never vibrate are the saddest chords of all.

My Father, prepare me for the place of Thy rest! I often speak as if the question were whether Thou wilt let me *in*. O no, that is not, that never was, the question! Thou hast never separated the good and the bad by locality. I doubt not that the wise and foolish virgins entered by the same *outward* gate; the door that was shut upon the foolish was an inward door. Hast Thou not told me that the man without the wedding garment got in with the white-robed multitude! It was after his *entrance* that he felt his want. I have no fear that I shall ever be driven from Thy presence; but I wish to enjoy that presence, to bask in it, to sing in it. I fear to stand by the crystal river and have no eye for its clearness. I dread to walk in the green pastures and have no sense of their richness. I am afraid to be at the concert of multitudinous voices and have no ear for their sweetness. I tremble to be enrolled in the league of pity and have no heart for its kindness. I dread not the thunder nor the earthquake nor the fire; I dread the circumstances of the blessed without their spirit of blessedness – the harp without the heart, the wing without the wish, the song without the soul, the labour without the love. Save me, O Father, from an uncongenial heaven!

Rests by the River

4. The Preparation of Man's Dwelling-Place

*"In My Father's house are many mansions . . .
I go to prepare a place for you."* John 14:2

We have here the telescope and the microscope.
The one reveals the vast places of the universe
– the many mansions of the Father; the other
fixes upon a unit in the void, "I go to prepare
a place for you." Often have I been startled by
the vastness of that sea in which my little life
is moving; I seem but a speck amid myriad
waves. Yet, it is not the distance that startles
me. If you could give me wings by which in a
moment I could reach the end of the universe,
it would not bring me one step nearer rest.

I want to know what *is* at the end of the
universe. Is there a human soul there? Is there
anything that can respond to my spirit? Is there
aught that can love when I love, weep when I
weep, joy when I joy? Is there a pulse of
sympathy that can answer to the pulse of my
heart? Is there a place prepared for me? I cannot
get that place by going over the bridge; I can
only get it by some one going over before me.
What I want is a heart already there, a kindred
soul to meet me, a human life to greet me. The
"going before" is itself the "preparing."

I want no gorgeous furniture in my room of
the Father's house. I am afraid the furniture may
be too gorgeous. I want something homely – like
home. I seek an old glance of the eye, an old ring
of the voice, an old clasp of the hand. I seek the
ancient sympathy that has linked man to man,
the earthly love that has knit heart to heart, the

human trust that has bound life to life. I seek in eternity the image of time; that is the place I would have prepared for me.

Searchings in the Silence

5. God's Dwelling-Place

"In Him dwelleth all the fulness of the Godhead bodily." Colossians 2:9

"Where does God live?" asks the little child; "Oh that I knew where I might find Him!" cries the earnest man. We are all seeking Thy dwelling-place, thou King of kings. We have not yet found a palace large enough to contain Thee. Some have sought Thee in the water, some in the air, some in the fire, because the water and the air and the fire are to us boundless things. Yet it is not in the boundless that Thou desirest to be found; it is in the limited, the broken, the contrite. The heaven of heavens cannot contain Thee, but the broken and the contrite heart can; it is there Thou delightest most to dwell.

Thy brightest glory is not in the stars, but in the struggles of a conquering soul. Thy temple is the heart of Him whom men have called the Man of sorrows. Thy fulness dwells in His emptiness, Thy wealth in His poverty, Thy strength in His weakness, Thy joy in His sorrow, Thy crown in His cross. Within that temple meet harmoniously the things which to the world are discords – perfection and suffering, peace and warfare, love and storm; the lion and the lamb lie down together.

There would I seek Thee, O my God. Within these sacred precincts, where all things are gathered into one, where middle walls of partition are broken down, where jarring chords are blended in one symphony of praise, there would I seek and find Thee. Under the shadow of that cross, where death meets life and earth is touched by heaven, my finite soul would lose its finitude and be one with Thee. My night would vanish in Thy day, my sorrow would melt in Thy joy, my meanness would merge in Thy majesty, my sin would be lost in Thy holiness. The veil which hides me from Thee is the shadow of my own will; when the veil of the temple shall be rent in twain I shall see the place where Thy glory dwelleth.

Moments on the Mount

6. The Preservation of Personality in the Christian Life

"That God may be all in all." 1 Corinthians 15:28

Am I, then, to be lost in God? Is my whole personal life to be absorbed and overshadowed in the light of the Infinite One? Am I to have no more separate being than one of those myriad drops which compose the vast ocean? If so, then my goal is death indeed. If my personality is to melt into the being of God as a cloud melts into the blaze of sunshine, then, surely, is God not my life but my annihilation. He can no longer say of me, "Because *I* live, thou shalt live also."

Nay, but, my soul, thou hast misread the destiny of thy being. It is not merely written that God is to be all, but that He is to be all *in* all. *His* universal life is not to destroy the old varieties of being; it is to pulsate through these varieties. His music is to fill the world, but it is to sound through all the varied instruments of the world. His sunshine is to flood the universe, but it is to be mirrored in a thousand various forms. His love is to penetrate creation, but it is to be reflected in the infinite diversities of the hearts and souls of men.

Thou speakest of losing thyself in the ocean of His love, but this is only poetically true. Love is an ocean where no man permanently loses himself; he regains himself in richer, nobler form. The only ocean in which a man loses himself is self-love; God's love gives him back his life that he may keep it unto life eternal.

Thou art not thyself until thou hast found God. Wouldst thou truly behold thyself? then must thou with open face behold as in a glass His glory. Thou wilt never become a power to thyself until God has become all in thee; thou wilt never really live until thou hast lived in Him.

Forget thyself, my soul. Forget thy pride and thy selfishness, thy cares and thy crosses, thy world which thou bearest within thee. Unbar the doors of thy being to the sunshine of that other Presence that already stands without, waiting to get in. And, verily, thy forgetfulness shall make thee strong, thy surrender shall make thee mighty, thy dying unto self shall make thee alive for evermore. Thy form shall be beautiful when it is gilded by His light, thy voice shall be melodious when it is tuned by His music, thy heart shall be on fire when it is quickened by His love; thou shalt be everything when God shall be all.

Moments on the Mount

7. Self-surrender

"If any man be in Christ, he is a new creature"
2 Corinthians 5:17

> O Love that wilt not let me go,
>   I rest my weary soul in Thee;
> I give Thee back the life I owe,
>   That in Thine ocean depths its flow
>   May richer, fuller be.

2 O Light that followest all my way,
>   I yield my flickering torch to Thee;
> My heart restores its borrowed ray,
>   That in Thy sunshine's blaze its day
>   May brighter, fairer be.

3 O Joy that seekest me through pain,
>   I cannot close my heart to Thee;
> I trace the rainbow through the rain,
>   And feel the promise is not vain
>   That morn shall tearless be.

4 O Cross that liftest up my head,
>   I dare not ask to fly from Thee;
> I lay in dust life's glory dead,
>   And from the ground there blossoms red
>   Life that shall endless be.

Sacred Songs